与大师对话

——中外英语名家访谈录

主　编 / 曾庆锴

副主编 / 张海港　彭　伦　王晓珊

上海外语教育出版社
SHANGHAI FOREIGN LANGUAGE EDUCATION PRESS

图书在版编目（CIP）数据

与大师对话：中外英语名家访谈录：汉、英 / 曾庆锴主编 . -- 上海：上海外语教育出版社，2023
ISBN 978-7-5446-7253-5

Ⅰ . ①与… Ⅱ . ①曾… Ⅲ . ①英语—教学研究—文集
Ⅳ . ① H319.3-53

中国国家版本馆 CIP 数据核字 (2023) 第 058176 号

出版发行：**上海外语教育出版社**
　　　　　（上海外国语大学内）　邮编：**200083**
电　　话：021-65425300 (总机)
电子邮箱：bookinfo@sflep.com.cn
网　　址：http://www.sflep.com
责任编辑：董　新

印　　刷：苏州工业园区美柯乐制版印务有限责任公司
开　　本：**710×1000　1/16**　印张 **11.25**　字数 **183** 千字
版　　次：2023 年 7 月第 1 版　2023 年 7 月第 1 次印刷

书　　号：ISBN 978-7-5446-7253-5

定　　价：**68.00** 元

本版图书如有印装质量问题，可向本社调换
质量服务热线：**4008-213-263**

编者的话

党的二十大擘画了中国式现代化的宏伟蓝图。二十大报告把教育、科技、人才提到"全面建设社会主义现代化国家的基础性、战略性支撑"的重要地位。在新征程上,如何培养满足新时代国家发展和民族复兴需要的英语人才,成为当前我国英语教育亟待解决的问题。

习近平总书记曾经指出:"推进教育现代化,要坚持对外开放不动摇,加强同世界各国的互容、互鉴、互通。"这为教育的对外开放指明了方向,国际交流和合作在我国教育事业中的地位和作用进一步凸显。自2018年以来,中国日报社联合上海外国语大学共同举办国际英语教育中国大会,为中外英语教育工作者搭建了一个国际化、专业性、高规格的交流平台,旨在推进英语教育国际交流与合作,以全球视野为中国英语教育建言,以中国智慧为全球英语教育献策。

2022年是国际英语教育中国大会举办五周年。五年来,百余位国内外英语教育领域的顶尖专家受邀做大会发言,涵盖英语教学理论、改革探索、教学实践、教学评估、教育技术等主题,充分体现了大会的前瞻性、引领性、专业性、启发性和包容性。许多专家接受我们的专访,分享其学术历程、研究成果和教育心得。这既是国际英语教育中国大会的宝贵财富,也是中国和世界英语教育的重要成果。

为纪念国际英语教育中国大会创办五周年,我们着手编辑出版《与大师对话——中外英语名家访谈录》一书,收录过去五年中部分参会中外专家的访谈稿,以飨读者。此项工作得到了专家们的大力支持。他们在繁忙的教学、科研工作之余抽出时间对采访稿件进行了认真修订,并结合时代发展补充了新内容。上海外语教育出版社孙玉社长对此书的出版高度重视,提出了大量专业意见;国际英语教育中国大会学术委员会专家梅德明教授为本书倾情作序,对国际英语教育中国大会的发展寄予厚望;责任编辑董新对所有文字及图片进行了细致的审订。在此,谨向所有促成此书出版的专家和上海外语教育出版社同仁表示衷心的感谢!

在新征程上,发展中国英语教育事业任重道远。我们希望通过此书的出版,与外语教育界同仁相互切磋,共同努力,为推动中国英语教育发展和中外英语教育交流助一臂之力,为建设教育强国做出一点贡献!

编者

2023 年 5 月 31 日

让中国走向世界，让世界了解中国

——国际英语教育中国大会的历史使命

（代序）

    国际英语教育中国大会创办于 2018 年，历经五届，已成为中国英语教育界举办的学术水平高、参与面广、国际影响力大的学术盛会，受到业界广泛关注和高度评价。

    国际英语教育中国大会于 2018 年 7 月 20 日在上海举行首次会议，之后确定杭州为每年一届的大会固定举办地。大会由中国日报社和上海外国语大学联合主办，旨在加强中国与世界在英语教育方面的对话与交流，为广大中外英语教育工作者搭建了相互学习、相互借鉴、相互切磋的学习与交流平台。这是一个高端、专业、国际化的学习与交流平台，与会代表在此分享英语教育理念、教学模式和人才培养经验，共谱新时代中国英语教育现代化的新篇章，同启人类命运共同体背景下文明交流互鉴的新征程。

    国际英语教育中国大会既是世界英语教育界了解中国英语教育的窗口，也是中国英语教育界立足时代、融通中外、沟通世界的桥梁，有助于促进中国英语教育与国际接轨，学习、借鉴其他国家先进的英语教育理念、教学方法、评价方式及教师培养模式，加强同国际英语教育界的交流与互动，提升中国英语教育的国际化水平；与此同时，通过广泛交流和深入研讨，展示我国英语教育改革取得的卓越成就，以中国经验、中国智慧、中国方案为全球英语教育建言献策，提升中国英语教育的国际地位和形象，促进构建全球英语教育共同体。海内外高校英语教育专家和学者、中小学英语教研员、一线英语教师以及教育管理工作者围绕特定主题及专门议题，以线上线下相结合的形式，通过主旨发言、专题研讨、微论坛、工作坊、课例展示、论文发言及论文张贴等丰富多彩的活动,分享英语教育领域的前沿研究成果和课堂教学实践案例。通过学术切磋、信息分享、经验交流、观点碰撞、思想交锋、共识达成,与会代表眼中有学子,心中有大爱,一切为了学生,为了一切学生,为了学生的成长和成才,为了学生走向世界、走向未来。

国际英语教育中国大会从第三届起开设了"一带一路"英语教育发展论坛,邀请来自不同国家的学者共同探讨"一带一路"背景下国际英语教育的新形势、新理念、新发展,旨在促进"一带一路"沿线国家和地区英语教育界的互动交流,为推动"一带一路"英语教育共同体的构建和发展提供积极、有效的平台支持和智力支撑,进而带动"一带一路"英语教育协同发展。

随着中国特色社会主义进入新时代,推动实现中华民族伟大复兴的中国梦的目标对中国英语教育提出了新的要求,构建人类命运共同体和"一带一路"倡议为中国英语教育提供了新的机遇。英语教育界应抓住机遇,以更高远的历史站位、更宽广的国际视野,朝着更高质量、更有效率、更加公平、更可持续的方向加快推进英语教育现代化。新时代的中国日益走近世界舞台中央,国际社会前所未有地关注中国、注视中国、倾听中国,外语人才特别是英语人才的需求不断凸显。英语是当今世界经济、政治、科技、文化等活动中广泛使用的主要语言媒介,是国际交流与合作的重要沟通工具,也是传播人类文明成果的主要载体之一,对中国走向世界、世界了解中国、构建人类命运共同体具有重要作用。中国的英语教育是国家整体战略的重要组成部分,为促进中国与世界对话交流、促进世界读懂中国发挥了不可替代的积极作用。国家和社会对英语教育事业提出了更高要求,要求英语教育界致力于推动中国英语教育事业发展,努力培养具有中国情怀、国际视野和跨文化交流能力的时代新人。

中国共产党第二十次全国代表大会要求"推进高水平对外开放",并明确表示:"中国坚持对外开放的基本国策,坚定奉行互利共赢的开放战略,不断以中国新发展为世界提供新机遇,推动建设开放型世界经济,更好惠及各国人民。"中国的英语教育工作者应该以新的更高站位,担当起新的历史责任,以习近平新时代中国特色社会主义思想为引领,坚持培根铸魂、启智增慧的人文教育价值取向,审视英语人才核心素养的培养目标,深化以英语课程为主要载体、以立德树人为根本任务、以学生成人成才为价值旨归的英语教学模式和学习方式的变革,加快推进英语教育现代化，推进中国英语教育事业不断创新发展，积极服务人才的全面成长，服务国家全面开放的新格局和扩大对外交流与合作的日益增长的需求，加强国际传播能力建设和国际传播人才培养，促进构建人类命运共同体，促进国际人文交流与合作，促进文明对话与互鉴。文明因多样而交流，因交流而互鉴，因互鉴而发展。语言是文化、文明交流的重要载体，英语教育界应该为开展不同文明之间的交流与对话、深化人文交流互鉴、促进中外有效沟通与合作、推动构建人类命运共同体做出贡献。

世界英语教师协会主席埃斯特尔·容（Ester J. de Jong）在首届国际英语教育中国大会发言时表明，英语教育进入了新领域，而这个领域就在中国。在新时代，英语教师要转变自身定位，既要让自己成为一名终身学习的实践者，又要让自己成为终身学习风潮的推动者。教学不再仅仅是教授学生知识或传授技能，而是要引导学生在这个信息爆炸的时代辨别知识的可靠性。语言也不再只是课本上的一条条语法规则，而是获取信息、表达自我、传递信息以及进行跨学科交流的媒介。在这个信息爆炸的新时代，我们需要的不再是单纯传授知识的老师，而是引路人、创新者、激励者，培养学生成为终身学习者。

我赞同埃斯特尔·容的观点。我认为，国际英语教育中国大会的一个重要意义是为中外英语教师提供了一个平台，一个各种思想碰撞、各种观念交流、各种成果分享的学习平台。国际英语教育中国大会的积极意义还在于，中国英语教育工作者通过参与这一学术水平高、参与面广、国际影响力大的学术盛会，有机会积极投身于构建英语教育国际共同体。国际英语教育中国大会在将世界朝我们拉近的同时，也积极推动着我们走向世界。

我以为，英语教育工作者应该进一步明确英语教育的学科特色和专业属性，以德立身，以德立学，以德施教，朝着高素质、专业化的目标，提升专业能力和育人质量。英语教育应该帮助学生在学习和掌握语言知识和语用技能的同时，树立家国情怀和文化自信，形成构建人类命运共同体所需要的情感、态度和价值观，弘扬全人类共同价值。学习英语不仅仅在于我们学什么，更在于我们学后能做什么。我们所处的世界是一个各国、各民族、各种文化相互关联的整体，这个相互关联的世界应该是一个互助和共享的世界，我们不仅要关注当地问题，更要关注全球问题和跨文化问题。我国英语教育必须回答培养什么人、如何培养人、为谁培养人这三个重要问题。我们的答案是:英语学科建设和英语课程教育必须致力于培养具有中国情怀、中国灵魂、国际视野、人类命运共同体意识、跨文化交流与合作能力的时代新人,他们具有语言能力、文化意识、思维品质、学习能力等英语学科素养,这也是我国英语与其他语种共享的"外语教育的大观念和公约数",统领我国外语教育的各个关键环节,包括课程理念、课程目标、课程内容、教学方法、学业评价以及教材建设和教师发展都要渗透共同体的观念和意识。未来的世界是一个不确定的世界,我们的学生有了上述情怀、视野、能力,就有了方向和定力,他们即使在前进过程中遇到艰难险阻,但是如果我们在英语教育的过程中帮助他们形成的正确价值观、必备品格和关键能力,就能使他们冲破艰难险阻,在走向未来的征程中终身受益。

我以为,我们的英语教育应该在帮助学生了解不同地区人民的生活方式、思维方式和文化传统,领悟世界文化的多样性、丰富性的同时,客观、理性、辩证地看待世界,形成正确的价值观、健康的审美情趣和道德情感,学会在未来的跨文化交流中坚守中国立场,用所学英语讲好中国故事、传播中华文化,主动积极地与来自多元文化背景的人们共同构建人类命运共同体。因此,在英语教学中融入中国情怀、国际视野和全球胜任力是时代赋予中国英语教育工作者的义不容辞的重要使命。我们应立足中国国情和现状,从时代发展的新需求出发,充分研究中国的英语学习者的特点及需求,深入了解中国的英语教育现状。中国的英语教育既要实现语言目标,又要实现文化目标,更要实现德育目标。为此,新时代中国英语教育要求英语教师在专业素质、学科知识和教学能力方面达到更高的境界,为英语教学改革提供根本保障。

我以为,我们要打造大中小学一条龙英语教育模式,各学段的英语课程规划都应体现学科核心素养和全球胜任力的发展,在各学段的英语教学中实现教育理念、课程理念、教学目标、课程设计、教学方法、评价体系、教师培训、教材与教学资源等方面的一致性和一体化。要坚持英语教学整体观,坚持中国情怀、全球关切、德育为魂、能力为重的育人理念,以学科核心素养和胜任能力为教学目标,采用先进的教育理念和教学方法,对英语课程内容的诸要素进行整合和融合,力求改变当前英语课堂语言知识讲解碎片化、单项类语言技能训练、输入与产出分离的教学现状,着力培养学生的语言能力、文化意识、思维品质和学习能力,并以此为枢轴,一以贯之地将核心素养发展体现在课程育人的各个环节。坚持英语教学整体观意味着主动变革英语课程的教学模式、学习方式、评价导向,要求教师主动设计、组织和实施一系列以学生为中心的学习活动,体现语言学习的综合性、进阶性、实践性特点,体现语言运用的工具性价值和人文性价值,体现学习理解、应用实践、迁移创新的基本环节和进阶要求。

我以为,进入新时代的中国英语教育应以立德树人为教育之坐标、教师之使命、学人之追求。学生为本,品德为魂,素养为轴,能力为重;着重理想、本领、担当,培育"三有"新人。21世纪育英语人才,中国情怀、国际视野、跨文化沟通能力缺一不可,"中国情怀"乃国人之根基,"国际视野"乃学人之境界,"跨文化沟通能力"乃育人之使命。旨在发展学生核心素养的中国英语教育以语言能力为基础要素,文化意识为价值取向,思维品质为心智特征,学习能力为发展条件。学科核心素养之形成,由表及里,由内而外。学科核心素养之发展,启智今人,惠及来者。国际英语教育中国大会致力于推动培育和发展英语学习者的核心素养,助力培养具有中国情怀、国际视野和跨文化沟通能力的时代新人,对我国英语课程育人事业做出了重要贡献。

中国英语教育界以育人为本,明德启智,明德尚行,问道习术,以道载术。中国英语教育界同仁不偏识外国语言、外国文化、外国故事,一定坚守中国立场,弘扬中国精神,传播中华文化,讲好中国故事。中华文明五千年之凝练妙合,钩深致远,体现着当代中华民族所持人类命运共同体之理念。中华文化洋溢着沁人心脾的人文精神,折射出光芒耀眼的人本思想,积淀着中华民族之精神追求、道德理念和行为规范。中华文化融理念、智慧、气魄、神韵于一炉,既是中华民族自信自豪之源泉,也是中外交流合作之内涵。"信之所以为信者,道也。""道者,恒也。"培根铸魂、启智增慧是中国英语教育的永恒之道,这是信奉天下苍生的共存之道,是笃信人类命运的共通之道,是追求成人成事的共为之道。

呈现在读者面前的这部《与大师对话——中外英语名家访谈录》旨在体现国际英语教育中国大会倡导的英语教育共同体所秉持的"永恒之道""共存之道"和"共为之道"。《访谈录》记载了中国日报社记者与应邀参与历届国际英语教育中国大会的部分国内外英语教育界专家学者所作的精彩访谈和生动交流。《访谈录》是"让中国走向世界,让世界了解中国"的生动写照,忠实地记录了驰骋于英语教育领域的各路领军人物对国际国内英语教育理论与实践的真知灼见,展现了新时代英语教育培根铸魂、启智增慧的中国方案,谱写了中外英语教育工作者携手共建英语教育命运共同体的华丽篇章。《访谈录》容各家之理,纳众人之言,无愧前贤,惠及后人,殊堪嘉勉。《访谈录》点亮智慧灯,鸣响启航笛,开启新征程,谱写新篇章,对立德树人的永恒使命做出了庄严的承诺。

中国共产党第二十次全国代表大会要求增强中华文明传播力、影响力。习近平总书记在二十大报告中提出,要"坚守中华文化立场,提炼展示中华文明的精神标识和文化精髓,加快构建中国话语和中国叙事体系,讲好中国故事,传播好中国声音,展现可信、可爱、可敬的中国形象。……深化文明交流互鉴,推动中华文化更好走向世界。"新时代的中国英语教育工作者要牢记肩负的新使命,胸怀天下,自信自强,守正创新,踔厉奋发,勇毅前行,立足"两个大局"对新时代人才培养提出的新要求,致力于铸魂育人,致力于推动构建人类命运共同体,致力于提升国家文化软实力和中华文化影响力、提升国际传播效能、深化文明交流互鉴、让中国走向世界、让世界了解中国。

是为序。

梅德明

上海外国语大学

2022 年 10 月 31 日

目 录

第一部分

中国专家访谈录

查明建

查明建,博士,教授,博士生导师,上海外国语大学副校长,兼任第八届国务院学位委员会外国语言文学学科评议组召集人、中国译协副会长、上海市外文学会会长、教育部重大课题攻关项目首席专家。主要研究方向为比较文学与世界文学理论、翻译文学研究、中外文学关系研究。著作有《中国 20 世纪外国文学翻译史(1898—2000)》(上、下卷)、《一苇杭之:查明建教授讲比较文学与翻译研究》等。译著有《比较文学批评导论》《什么是世界文学?》等。

提高英语专业人文学科地位是
高等外语教育的重要任务

上海外国语大学查明建教授专访

记者：一直以来，国内高校英语教育普遍存在中国文化失语现象，"中国文化失语症"的主要原因是什么？ 具体有哪些表现？

查明建：这个问题问得好！ 当代外语教育有个较大的缺失，就是不甚重视学生中国语言文化能力的培养，认为这不是外语专业的教育内容。我想主要原因，一是外语教育理念方面的问题，比较孤立地看待外语学习，认为外语教育就是学习外语，与母语文化没什么关系。二是没有很好地理解母语文化能力之于外语学习的助益作用，以及它对于丰富外语专业人才培养内涵的意义。

关于英语教育中的中国文化缺失，据我观察，主要表现在以下几个方面：一是在语言教学中，缺乏英汉语在语法、表达习惯以及语言背后思维方式的比较意识。二是在专业课程中，如英美文学、英美文化、英美概况等课程中，缺乏跨文化比较意识，即不善于与中国文学、中国文化联系起来，作中外比较。如果有较强的跨文化比较意识，将相关问题有机地与中国文化联系起来进行比较、分析，引导学生思考中西文化的特点、特质，并对形成这些特质的原因进行思考，就能激发学生自主性学习、思考，课外带着问题做专题性阅读，久而久之，学生的文化视野就打开了。有了对中西文化比较深入的了解和理解，将来从事涉外工作，就有了较好的中外文化修养和从事专业领域工作的知识基础。三是外语教育的立意问题。我们的外语教育，目的是培养外语学科领域的研究型人才和应用型涉外人才，广泛学习世界先进文化和文明成果,服务于国家文化、文明建设,做到文明互鉴,促进中外文化交流和中国文化国际传播。如果我们对自己的母语文化都不熟悉,就很难胜任相关的工作。不能说我们是中国人,就必然了解中国文化,必然领会中国文化的内涵。中国文化博大精深,我们日常生活中所接触、所熟悉的,只是中国文化某些物化形态的东西,这些只是中国文化的外在表现形式,其内在的哲学、思想、精神,仍需要一个学习、研读、理解、消化、体认的过程。

外语教育如果忽视提高学生的中国语言文化修养,其结果就是:学生的外语水平可能比较高,但中文能力比较弱,对中国文化没有深切的体认,以后就很难发挥中外文化交流方面的作用,也很难做好涉外工作。现在提出来英语教育中的中国文化缺失问题,确实应该引起我们的高度重视,促使我们有意识地在专业教育中补上这一块,从而培养出英语精通同时又熟知自己母语文化、真正能进行跨文化沟通的人才。

记者:为何说母语水平在相当程度上是外语学习的助推器?

查明建:母语语言文化是一个人心智发展的基础,直接关系到他/她的思维能力、思想能力、想象能力和学习能力。资中筠先生认为,一个人的文化程度和文化修养,是由一个人的母语文化修养所决定的。她深有体会地说:"一个国家的母语是它文化的载体。你学了多少,你掌握了多少母语,你就会成为有什么样文化修养的人。""我是学外文专业出身的,我从小学就开始学外文,专业学的是英国文学,但是到今天我也不认为,学不学英国文学能够决定我的文化程度。我的文化程度还是我的中文决定的,我的思辨和表达能力取决于中文。"[1]王佐良先生指出:"汉语学得好的,外语也容易学好,特别是到了稍高的阶段是这样。写文章的道理是共通的,需要大量文史、科技知识也是共通的;而这一切之上,需要有丰富、灵活的想象力更是共通的。"[2]这些都是经验之谈。可见,母语和母语文化是滋养一个人"丰富、灵活的想象力"的源头活水。

当年清华大学外文系就非常重视中国语言文学。吴宓先生执笔的《清华大学外国语文学系概况(1934)》中就强调:"本系对学生选修他系之学科,特重中国文学系。盖中国文学与西洋文学关系至密。"因为无论是为了"(一)创造中国之新文

---

① 资中筠:《文化要用母语讲》,《国学》2010年第10期,第4页。
② 王佐良:《外语教育往事谈——教授们的回忆》,上海:上海外语教育出版社,1988年,第227页。

学,以西洋文学为源泉为圭臬;或(二)编译书籍,以西洋之文明精神及其文艺思想,介绍传布于中国;又或(三)以西文著述,而传布中国之文明精神及文艺于西洋,则中国文学史学之知识修养,均不可不丰厚。故本系注重与中国文学系相辅以行者可也"。①

外语界的一些名家学者,如吴宓、钱锺书、季羡林、杨宪益、杨周翰、许国璋、王佐良等,他们既是杰出的外国文学专家、语言学家、翻译家,同时又有极高的中国文化修养。他们之所以能成为这样的学贯中西的大家,归功于他们早年打下的中国语言文化功底。从外语界前辈的身上,我们得到很大启示:一个人的母语水平与外语学习能力关系密切。我们的理解力、想象力、审美能力、情感能力、思辨能力,首先都是从母语语言文化中获得的。我们的母语文化帮助我们开发了心智,提升了心智的境界。有了较高的母语文化修养和较强的母语运用能力,借助于母语语言文化经验去学习外语,外语也会学得更好。

记者:高校英语教育应如何把中国文化融入英语教学中,从而让学生在学习外语的同时提高母语文化功底?

查明建:我认为,比较文学有助于提高英语专业学生的中国文化修养。"比较文学与跨文化研究"已确立为外语学科的五大方向之一;教育部高等学校外国语言文学类专业教学指导委员会编制的《普通高等学校本科外国语言文学类专业教学指南》中,也建议英语专业开设比较文学相关课程,如"中外文化比较""比较文学导论""中外比较文学研究专题""中外人文交流研究专题""跨文化研究专题"等。这些课程对提高英语专业学生人文修养、培养跨文化比较意识有极大的作用。就增强学生中国语言文化修养而言,比较文学涉及中外文学比较,其前提就是不仅要读外国文学作品,更要读中国文学作品。英语专业开设比较文学相关课程,可促使学生加强中国文学和文化典籍的阅读,在阅读中体会中文之优美和中国文化之深邃。

此外,在英语教学中应有跨文化比较意识。可借鉴和灵活运用比较文学的方法,如在语言基础课程教学中,有意识地引导学生将英语与汉语的语法、结构、表达方式等进行对比,增强对英汉语言特点的认识。语言是文化的载体。语言所表现出来的特点,深刻地反映了文化的特点和不同文化中人的思维方式。在文化的维

---

① 吴宓:《清华大学外国语文学系概况(1934)》,(原载《清华周刊》第41卷第13、14期合刊,1934年6月1日),转引自吴宓《世界文学史大纲》,商务印书馆,2020年,第444页。

度中进行英汉语比较,可在民族文化和文化心理更深的层面上引导学生进一步思考中英思维方式、审美方式、修辞方式和表达方式,发现共性和差异。这样,英语教学就增加了中国文化的内涵。

在其他知识类课程,如西方思想经典导读、中国思想经典导读、西方文明史、西方礼仪文化等课程教学中,有机地运用比较文学方法,将中外相关方面的内容进行互参、互识,引导学生思考中外差异和跨文化沟通问题,可激发他们带着问题去做研究性阅读,这样可加深对中国文化的理解。对中国文化有较深入的理解,才能以地道的英语、合适的话语方式去讲述中国文化,讲述中国故事。

记者:您曾提到,英语专业要提升在人文学科中的专业地位,就必须在专业理论、人才培养目标、课程体系建设、教学模式等方面进行全面而深刻的改革。目前上外英语学院在上述领域实施了哪些行之有效的措施?成果如何?

查明建:过去受英语学习条件限制,学生入学英语水平较低,只能在本科阶段强化学生的语言技能训练,从大一到大四基本上都是听说读写译之类的课程。长期的以英语语言技能训练为中心的教学模式造成了人们对英语专业的严重误解,误以为英语专业就是学英语的专业。这实际上混淆了英语学习与英语专业学习、英语教育与英语专业教育的本质区别。

英语专业作为人文学科门类中的一个专业,有其学科属性要求和特定的专业内涵。英语专业与中文专业一样,都属于人文学科。既然中文专业不是狭义的学习中文的专业,那么英语专业也不是仅仅学英语的专业。掌握英语语言能力,是英语专业的基本要求,是进入专业学习的语言能力准备,而不是专业学习的全部内容。

要提升英语专业在人文学科中的地位,就要坚守英语专业的人文学科性质和专业本位,坚定专业价值信念,加强专业内涵建设,按专业所要求的人才培养目标来设置课程体系、改革教学方式、提升教学的专业化和人文化品质,培养出高质量的专业人才,满足国家对高层次英语专业人才的需要,彰显英语专业人才培养的社会意义和价值。

为此,上海外国语大学英语专业自 2010 年着手进行"人文化"教育改革,强化英语专业的人文学科意识和专业建设意识,提出"英语专业不是学英语的专业,而是通过英语来学习人文社科知识,培养英语精通的人文领域专业人才"的理念,以培养英语精通、专业功底扎实、人文素养深厚、思辨能力和创新能力强的通识型、通用型英语专业人才为目标，以人文化、专业化、国际化为导向，从专业理念、课程体系到教学模式、教师发展等方面进行综合改革。所谓"人文化"，就是针对过去片面强调英语专业学习的实用性、工具性，而坚持英语专业的人文学科性质和人文教育理念，按照人文学科内涵的要求，开阔学生的人文视野，建立比较完善的人文知识结构，为专业学习和今后的事业发展奠定比较扎实的人文知识基础。所谓"专业化"，就是针对过去以语言技能训练为中心的教学模式，坚持英语专业教育的内涵式发展，按专业人才的培养要求，建立专业的知识体系，在课程体系设置上体现专业学习的内涵和特点。

英语专业教育人文化改革是个综合性工程，我们将课程体系改革作为切入点和抓手，优化原有课程，以英语专业卓越人才的培养为目标，打造充分体现人文性和专业性、具有系统性和进阶性的课程体系。

新的课程体系，对原有的专业选修课程，一是进行优化，如将"古希腊罗马神话赏析"改为"古希腊罗马神话与西方文化"，以提升课程的人文内涵和学术品格。二是完善英语专业人文通识课程体系，对原有欧美文化、文学、语言学、翻译四大板块的选修课程进行扩充，开设"比较文学导论""中西文化比较""英语史""欧洲文化入门""西方哲学精华""西方文明史""英美历史""英美社会与文化""文化研究入门""社会问题圆桌讨论""西方艺术史"等课程。三是增加两个板块的系列课程："人文社会科学原著导读"系列和"中国文化"（英文）系列讲座。

新的课程体系确定后，就是抓教学改革。我们提出要开展"研究性教学"。所谓"研究性教学"，就是改变过去教师讲、学生听的知识灌输型的填鸭式教学方式，而是以问题为导向，启发学生思考，激励学生在课外多阅读，拓展知识面，扩大人文视野，培养思辨能力和思想方法。

如《英美社会与文化》之类的课程教学，教学重点不是向学生介绍英美历史、英美社会文化的常识性内容，而在于启发学生思考：英美历史、英美社会文化为什么会如此发展，其文化基因是什么？哪些基因性质的文化因素对后来的发展起到了决定性的作用？这些基因性的文化因素在社会发展、变迁中又出现了哪些变异，体现在哪些社会现象中？等等。总之，此类课程需从具体的文化现象事例入手，通过分析英美社会、文化的形态，进而进入文化特质和民族特性（国民性）的探讨。

而分析文化特质和民族特性,自然离不开对历史形成原因的分析。在合适的地方,还可相机与中国文化的相关情况进行比较。通过这种从现象到本质、从外到内、宏微互参的研究型、启发式的教学方式,引导学生从掌握常识、了解现象到发现问题,继而进入研究型的思考、分析,以此培养学生的学术能力和思维能力。

上外英语专业教育人文化改革至今已有十年,十年来的努力取得了令人满意的成效。英语专业人文化教育改革在全国英语界都得到同行们的广泛认同。经常有外校的同行来上外英语学院观摩教学,问询我们英语专业人文化改革的经验。我在学生身上也看到了人文化教育改革后的可喜变化。高中毕业生被英语专业的课程所吸引,报考英语专业的第一志愿率明显上升,优质生源又回到了英语专业。在校学生的人生立意也提高了。他们的人生理想,不再是谋个高薪职业,而是从谋职业转向了谋事业。这是最令人高兴的事,因为我们之所以付出这么多努力进行英语教育改革,就是为了培养有事业心的高质量外语专业卓越人才,为国家和社会发展做出英语专业的贡献。

值得一提的是,我们基于拔尖创新人才应从本科抓起的理念,在人文化改革取得成效的基础上,于2018年又创建了"人文社会学科研究型人才培养实验班"(简称"人文实验班"),希望通过"人文实验班"加大专业拔尖创新人才培养的力度,探索高端化、精英化、专业化人才的培养机制,通过实验班的人才培养创新模式和标杆作用,整体提升学院人才培养的水平,打造一流本科,培养更多的高端专业人才,引领全国英语专业的创新发展。

记者:您提到钱锺书、季羡林等大家,为何那一代的很多学者母语和外语水平都很高?

查明建:钱锺书、季羡林、杨宪益、许国璋、王佐良那一代学者,他们在小学、中学阶段都受过很好的国文教育。他们在少儿时代就熟读、背诵古代经典名篇,奠定了中文功底和文学修养,为他们后来的外语学习奠定了基础。他们外语水平高与其早年外语学习方法有关系。一个人中文好,不是靠背生词、背字典、背语法条文学好的,而是靠大量阅读,由简易读物到原著,由浅入深。中文学习方法可以用到外语学习上来,也就是说,怎样学中文,就怎样学外语。多读经典、名篇,从大量阅读中接触丰富、复杂的语言现象,一点点感受,一点点体会,日积月累,语感和语言能力就自然而然提高了。学语言,要像学游泳,首先要下水,让水包围着自己,在水里感知、感受、感悟水性,在水中学会游泳,而不是天天在岸上背诵、琢磨游泳手册。

记者:那个年代并没有那么多外语教育理论和方法,也没有先进的硬件条件和外语学习软件,为什么西南联大能培养出如此多的外语人才? 我国的外语教育有哪些优秀传统可资借鉴?

查明建:这确实是个耐人寻味的现象。论外语学习条件,那个年代远不能跟现在相比;论教学方法,那时谈不上有什么系统的外语教育理论和教学法,也很少有人专门去研究外语教学法,基本上就是教师根据自己的外语学习经验来教学。据当年的清华、西南联大学生回忆,无论是吴宓、叶公超、陈福田,还是钱锺书,似乎都不大讲解词汇和语法,更不会讲解生词含义,认为这是学生在课前应该自己去查阅、掌握的。他们注重的是课文里的措辞、语言背后的文化内涵,是语言与作者思想、情感的关系,即这样的语言表达了怎样的思想、情感,作者的思想情感又是通过怎样的语言形式来传达的,达到了什么效果。学生就在这样的教学中,感受到了语言的魅力和微妙之处,体会到语言与文化、语言与思想和情感的关系。许国璋、王佐良先生都是西南联大的学生。许国璋先生说:"我教学生从来不以教会他们几句英语或教会一种本事为目标,而是教会怎样做人。英语教育是用英语来学习文化、认识世界、培养心智,而不是英语教学。"王佐良先生说:"通过文化来学习语言,语言也会学得更好。"我想,他们这种语言学习观和外语教育观,正是他们受到早年西南联大老师们外语教学方式的影响,才有感而发的。

说到我国外语教育有哪些优秀传统可资借鉴,我想最当借鉴的,就是二三十年代清华和西南联大的外语教育理念。以《西南联大英文课》为例,这本教材是外文系主任陈福田教授编选的,西南联大所有专业的大一学生都共同学习这本英语教材。教材的编选给我们很大的启发,也引发我们的诸多反思。从编选上看,这本教材所选篇目可分为几大类:其一,"人文教育篇",包括伯特兰·罗素的《教育的目的》("What Shall We Educate for?")、托马斯·亨利·赫胥黎的《通识教育》("A Liberal Education")、约翰·亨利·纽曼的《什么是大学?》("What Is a University?")等。其二,"思想、思辨篇",选了查尔斯·W.艾略特的《对生活的持久满足》("The Durable Satisfactions of Life")、里拉·雷姆森的《何为科学?》("What Is Science?")、阿伯特·劳伦斯·洛维尔的《自由与约束》("Liberty and Discipline")、塞缪尔·麦考德·克罗瑟斯的《人人想当别人》("Every Man's Natural Desire to Be Somebody

Else"）。其三，"文学、人文情怀篇"，有赛珍珠的《贫瘠的春天》（"Barren Spring"）、威廉·萨默塞特·毛姆的《负重的牲口》（"Beast of Burden"）、《河之歌》（"Song of the River"）、胡适的《乐观看中国》（"An Optimist Looks at China"）等。课文后的练习，都是紧扣课文内容的问题。这些问题需要学生吃透课文、深入思考才能回答出来。这些练习使学生在学以致用的同时还培养了思想能力。

《西南联大英文课》充分体现了西南联大的人文教育理念和外语教育理念，通过美文、经典名篇来学外语，通过外语学习来涵养学生的人文情怀与人文精神，培育思想能力。这样的教育，才真正体现了外语教育的立意！这样的外语学习，就超越了一般的外语教学，而让学生在学习外语的同时，有了更多的收获。这些东西在他们之后的生命中，会潜移默化地在内心中产生一种力量，不断激励自己向前走，向上、向善、向美！

窥斑见豹，从《西南联大英文课》我们可以看出当年外语教学的优胜之处：一是外语教育的理念——外语学习不能仅是学习语言，而要与语言所承载的文化一起来学。二是"取法乎上"，选择经典、美文来教学生学习外语。因为经典就是经典，是一种语言最美妙、最精致、最贴切、最能体现文化意味的表达。

龚亚夫

龚亚夫，中国教育科学研究院研究员，中国教育学会外语教学专业委员会理事长。长期从事中小学英语教育。自1988年起参加中英合编初中英语教材，参加编写、改编、主编数套中小学英语教材，其中包括《PEP小学英语》《新目标英语》《新维度英语》等。出版《任务型语言教学》《英语教育新论：多元目标英语课程》，发表有关英语教育的文章数十篇。研究领域包括交际语言教学、任务型语言教学、第二语言习得、英语课程设计以及教师教育等。

重新认识英语教育的三大目标

中国教育学会外语教学专业委员会理事长龚亚夫专访

记者：在全球化背景下，国内英语学习的热度一直上升，越来越多的孩子从小就接受英语教育。您认为学习英语的核心价值是什么？

龚亚夫：我觉得学习英语最核心的价值还是培养能交流的人，也就是说，其实我们教给孩子的不仅仅是一种能和别人交流的工具，我们教给孩子的还是一种思维的习惯，一种解决问题的能力，我觉得可能这是我们学习英语的核心价值。

学习英语的价值还可以从三个方面来看。第一，学习一门外语对人的大脑发育是有好处的，因为人的大脑并不是一块胶泥，而更像是一块肌肉。学习外语显然会增加学生的负担，也就是说给大脑增加了一个锻炼的机会，所以学习外语可以促进人的大脑发育。第二，学习外语可以帮助我们发展思维能力。比如，汉语和英语的表达方式有很大区别，当我们学习英语的时候，我们思维的逻辑性会更强，更加有缜密性。也就是说，我们学习一门外语的时候，我们换了一种思维方式，这对我们思维的发展也是有好处的。第三，学习外语对发展人的品格也有好处。我们现在都在讲，要实现立德树人根本任务，要培养学生的核心素养，要培养学生的必备品格和关键能力，那么学习外语实际上就是在学习和人交流，这对人的品格发展是有好处的。我们要学会换位思考，要学会如何正确地与别人打交道，要学习怎么样和别人交流才能更加成功等等，这些对我们的品格、对我们全方位地思考问题、对我们形成更多的包容性，都有非常大的好处。

记者：您怎样看待许多学习者追求"地道的"英语语音的现象？

龚亚夫：每一个以英语为母语的国家，它们的发音其实都是不一样的。美国、英国、加拿大、澳大利亚、新西兰，再加上一些所谓的外围的英语国家，它们之间的发音都不一样。所以，从这个意义上来说，发音其实并不是影响交流的最重要因素。我想，语调、连读、节奏，还有习惯用法，就是我们经常说的语块，可能是影响交流的更重要因素。

记者：我们的核心素养框架与国外相比有哪些特色？

龚亚夫：我们现在提倡的培养学生的核心素养和国外讲的人的全面发展、关键能力、国际理解力等等，从本质上来说是一样的。比如，中国传统文化中有"仁""义""礼""智""信"，我认为国外所讲的培养学生的品格、情感和我们讲的"仁""义""礼""智""信"实际上是一样的。我们这次大会提到了要融通中外，我觉得这一点从任务型语言教学来说就是一个很好的能融通中外的途径。

记者：在新课标、新课程、新教材在全国各地实施的大背景下，您认为英语学科如何才能通过教学实现核心素养的培养？

龚亚夫：国家教材局的申继亮博士讲过，我们的学科教学要超越学科，超越教材，超越课堂。我认为我们可以从这句话来理解英语教育。我们现在的教学目标发生了根本性的变化。过去，我们重点培养学生的语言运用能力，包括听说读写技能、语言知识，也包括一些思维方式、文化意识等等。而现在我们的教学目标发生了根本性变化，或者说我们对英语教育价值的认识发生了根本性变化。

我们现在认为，人和人之间的沟通交流不仅仅是语言的问题，也不仅仅是听说读写技能的问题，它还包括人的思维方式、价值观念、行为习惯、伦理道德、解决问题的能力等等，这些也就是人们常说的必备品格和关键能力。如果我们从这个角度去思考英语教育的价值，就会重新确定我们的教学目标、教学内容、教学路径、教学方法、教学资源、测试评价等等。我们需要综合考虑英语教育如何培养人的必备品格和关键能力，也就是促进人的全面发展，以此为目标去设计教学活动、教学方法和测评方法。

记者：现在不少英语教师在教授语言的同时，也非常注重培养学生的批判性思维和创造性，您能否阐述一下您所提倡的语言交流目标、思维认知目标、社会文化目标这三大英语教育目标？

龚亚夫：是的，我现在把英语教育的目标定位为三个，叫作多元目标。过去，我们主要考虑的是语言运用的目标，也就是说，我们主要考虑怎么样教会学生掌握一种外语。现在我把它设定为这三个目标。第一个是社会文化目标，主要是学生的品格培养，包括各种知识、全球意识等等。第二个是思维认知目标，主要是教给学生一种思维方式和一种认知方式。思维认知目标又包括三个方面：一个是正向的思维方式。我们知道，现在我们培养学生，不仅仅是培养他们一种认知的批判性思维能力、分析能力等等，我们同时还要培养学生正向的思维方式，或者说叫作成长的思维方式，这一点对于学生今后的发展来说也是非常重要的；另外就是学习策略和学习能力，也属于思维认知的这个目标中的一个成分；再有就是我们传统上说的语言学习的目标。第三个是语言交流目标。

这三个目标之间的关系是什么呢？当我们在和人们进行交流的时候，这三者之间实际上是密不可分的。也就是说，当我们和别人交流时，我们的思维方式、我们的品格和我们使用的语言，这三者之间是紧密相连的。比如，当我们跟别人说话的时候，我们如果能对别人很宽容，对别人很友善，实际上，这既是一种思维的方式，也是一种品格。当我们和别人交流的时候，我们把这三者用英语表达出来，但同时加上我们的行为习惯和一些同别人交流的体态语言等等，这三个点之间就构成了语言交流的这样的过程。所以，这就是三个多元目标的内涵。

记者：从您个人的经验来说，您认为学习英语对于个人成长和未来发展有何重要意义？

龚亚夫：我觉得从我自己学习外语的过程来说，它实际上首先给我们打开了一扇窗户，去认识世界，去认识世界上不同的人，我想这是一个很重要的方面。通过这个窗口，我们接触到了世界各国的一些文化、风土人情、思维方式等等，我想这些对于一个人的成长来说是很重要的。也就是说，我们不局限于自己原先生活的环境中去思考，我们会站到一个世界的角度来去看整个世界；同时，也从世界的角度来看我们的中国，看我们个人的成长，所以我觉得这可能是我认为学习外语对我个人来说的一个最大的好处。

记者：您认为英语教育工作者能从国际英语教育中国大会中收获什么？

龚亚夫：我觉得国际英语教育中国大会是一个非常独特的会议，因为通常来说，中小学老师开会的时候基本上都是中小学老师参加，而大学老师开会的时候基本上是在大学做研究的教授、学者们参加，所以这两个群体的人其实大部分情况下是很少有交叉的，或者说很少有交流。我想，作为大学的外语教育工作者，作为研究外语教学的人，应该更多地了解中小学教师的想法、困难和需求，这样他们才能说他们谈论的是中国的英语教育。而中小学老师平常所接触的都是和他们日常教学比较密切的东西。如果能有这样的一个机会，让他们可以了解到很多应用语言学的研究理论或者其他的语言学习理论，从而可以从理论的高度去认识自己的教学，认识自己的教学方法，去认识我们的教材，都是非常有好处的。

鲁子问

鲁子问，博士，教授，博士生导师，中国教育技术协会中小学外语信息化应用工作委员会主任。先后在湖北省秭归县陕西营中学、华中师范大学、加拿大卡尔顿大学、兴义民族师范学院工作，主要从事教师教育、民族教育、英语教育、跨文化教育研究与教学；出版学术专著十多部，编写大中小学教材十多套，获得国家教材一等奖、二等奖；长期坚持在中小学和民族地区开展课堂教学实践和全民阅读推动工作。

乡村英语教育发展的理由与路径

兴义民族师范学院鲁子问教授专访

记者：您如何看待近年来我国农村英语教育的发展？

鲁子问：这些年来，随着脱贫攻坚战略的实施与胜利完成，乡村教育有了很大的变化，乡村的英语教育也开始有了很大的发展。比如，现在我们看到，班班通已经基本实现，很多乡村小学在教室里能够直接使用互联网技术甚至 AI 技术来促进学生的英语学习。这得感谢国家现在对乡村基础教育设施的政策倾斜。

不过，在乡村英语教师配置，尤其是乡村小学英语教师的配置方面，还需要国家有更多的政策倾斜。现在我们有很好的特岗教师计划，但是真正英语专业毕业的特岗教师还是太少。我们也看到国家有很好的"银龄"计划，就是让刚刚退休的 60~65 岁的优秀教师到乡村支教，但是这一计划中的英语老师还是太少。我们希望，在英语促进教育公平这个层面上，有更多的政策出台，来支持乡村英语教育的发展，支持乡村英语教师的专业发展。

我们也都特别感谢中国日报社和 21 世纪英语教育传媒这些年来对乡村英语教育的关注。《21 世纪英语教育》曾连续十多期发表我们关于乡村英语教育的文章。我们也曾经随着中国日报社和 21 世纪英语教育传媒到贫困地区去开展教育扶贫。我们希望这样的扶贫有更多的人参与，不仅仅是一家报社、一个机构在做这样的事情，而是全社会共同来促进乡村英语教育的发展。

记者：有不少农村学生和家长仍然认为，在农村环境中英语没有实际用途。您怎么看待农村地区"英语无用论"这个问题？

鲁子问：若我们单从语言知识与技能角度学英语,的确,对于很多乡村学生来说,英语语言知识和技能是无用的,可能除了考试,几乎一辈子都不用英语。其实,英语知识和技能不仅对乡村学生"无用",对城市学生同样"无用"。

在基础教育阶段,每个学生都必须学习英语,乃至语文、数学、物理、化学等所有学科,而学习这些学科的过程有助于发掘和培养学生的潜能。

基础教育的绝大多数学科知识和技能其实都是终身无用的。我们都学过写议论文,可能除了考试,我们中很多人一辈子没写过议论文。我们都学过二元二次方程,可能除了考试,一辈子没用过二元二次方程;我们学了牛顿力学三定律,可能除了考试,一辈子没用过这些定律。

基于当前的个人潜能发现技术与人才选拔技术,中小学生要从三百六十行中筛选出自己长大后可以谋生与发展的学科与领域,国家要为每一学科领域筛选出具有该学科领域发展潜质的所需人才,就需要每一个学生在基础教育阶段都学习所有学科,然后进行必要的考试。每一个人其实最终基本上都只是在某一学科谋生与发展,也基本上只是在某一学科领域成为被国家筛选出来的人才,而其他学科领域都被我们自己筛下去;在其他学科领域,我们也被国家筛下去。基于目前的技术,不学习尽可能多的学科,不考试,就没法完成这一自我筛选和国家筛选。当然,未来人的潜能识别技术发展了,这一筛选可能更早一些。但在目前,这一筛选最起码要到九年义务教育结束才能基本完成。这是我们个人筛选谋生与发展潜能和国家筛选学科领域人才不得不付出的代价。英语如此,语文如此,数理化都是如此;乡村如此,城市亦如此。也就是说,我们自己需要这个学科潜能蓄水池供我们自己筛选,国家也需要这个人才蓄水池供国家筛选。

乡村学生占我国学生总数的一半以上。我国大批人才来自乡村,乡村是国家人才蓄水池的重要组成部分,英语人才亦然。若乡村学校不开设英语课程,乡村学生不学习英语,国家人才蓄水池的蓄水量就减少了一半以上,可能因此错失了一大批来自乡村的英语人才。

当然,基础教育当下的这种筛选方式的成本很高,因为我们基础教育阶段所学学科知识与技能,绝大部分我们一辈子都不会使用,或者很少使用。如何使这一筛选有更大效益,倒是我们可以努力改变的。我们应该使英语乃至各个学科都有除了运用学科知识与能力之外的"用"。这也就是现在确定学科核心素养的价值所在,学生在基础教育阶段不再以学科知识和技能为主,而以学科核心素养为主。当然,由于各种原因,现在的学科核心素养还存在一定的不足。以英语学科为例,其实跨文化认知素养更加重要,对个人和国家作用最大,我们有理由期待其成为英语学科核心素养的重点内容。

除了考试、国际交往与旅行之外,英语首先可以拓展我们的视野,让我们可以用英语这种视角认知这个世界。在这个意义上,学英语就是为我们自己打开了一扇门,或者架起了一座桥,让我们可以看得更广、更远、更多、更深,从与汉语不一样的视角拓展、丰富我们的认知,可以使我们少一些蒙昧,多一些敞明。

其次,学英语可以让我们了解更多道理、更多方法,形成更多智慧,从而使我们更有效地认识问题、分析问题、解决问题,从而更好地发展自己。比如我们要告诉来访者此地"闲人免进",其实来访者并非闲人,而是有事情而来,甚至与此处有一定关联,但若你知道这种表达的英文说法是 Staff only 或者 Authorised only,那你就可以直接告诉来访者,"此处是员工工作场所,非员工不可进入",或者"参观此地需要先行申请,获得批准后方可进入",来访者就会理解此时不可参观的理由。甚至使用英语本身,就可能帮助我们找到另一个解决问题的方法。比如当你两岁的尚不会英语的孩子哭闹着非要再吃一个冰淇淋时,若有人问你孩子为什么哭闹,你若直接说:"他已经吃了一个冰淇淋了,还要再吃一个",这时孩子听到了,肯定更加哭闹。但若你说"He wants another ice-cream.",就不会因为"冰淇淋"三个字刺激你的孩子更加哭闹。

第三,学英语可以让我们更好地反观自己,反观自己的文化,从而更广域、更深度地理解、认知自己和自己的文化。我经常举的一个例子是:我们每个人需要一面镜子,才能更清晰地看清楚自己的脸;没有镜子等对面反光物,我们根本无法看到自己的脸。比如,我们中国的长城在英语中被称为 the Great Wall of China,既没有"长",也没有"城",直译的语义是"中国大墙"。为什么呢? 首先,长城这一类功能的人造建筑在世界上很多,其性质属于 defensive wall(防御墙)。古希腊就在雅典建造了防御波斯军队的 the Long Walls,甚至伊朗也有一个 Great Wall,只不过是 the Great Wall of Gorgan;英国也有罗马皇帝哈德良时期建造的 Hadrian's Wall(哈德良长城,或者哈德良墙)。这些建筑现在都依然存在,如同我国的长城。其实这非常好地定义了我国长城的性质:防御。这说明我们是爱好和平的、不对外侵略的。当年西方传教士在介绍我国长城时,就直接使用了西方已有的 defensive wall 中的 wall 这一概念,至于 great 则是因为其的确 great。另外,我国之所以将长城称为"长城",是因为我国古代的城都是用墙围起来的城,而在长城的一些地方建有城,通常是关隘之城,并用墙连接起来。所以史书在早期多个概念并存之后不久,很早就确定了"长城"这一概念。显然,通过英语中对我国长城所用的名称——the Great Wall of China,我们既可以了解长城与世界很多民族防御性城墙的文化共性,也可以了解我国长城名称的由来,以及外国人对我国长城的赞美(great)。

当然,从哲学视角来看,无用本身也是一种用:无用之用。我国全体学生学英语,这本身就是我国坚持与深化对外开放的一个重要标志,既让全世界充分认同我国深化对外开放这一政策,也让全体国民充分理解和执行这一基本国策,促进全体国民形成对外开放的积极心态。这比有多少人学会了英语、未来是否运用英语都更加重要。这便是在国家社会层面最大的"无用之用",是哲学意义上的时代精神的"用"。

总之,英语对乡村孩子不仅有考试升学的"用",以及国际交往的"用"、出国留学与旅行等可能的"用",也有国家人才蓄水池的"用",更有拓展个人认知的"用",形成与发展时代精神的"用"。

尽管有人可能从个人视角会说乡村孩子有不学英语的权利,但作为中国国民,尤其是在教育经费由国家承担的当前政策下,学习英语是每个接受国家教育的人不可规避的义务,乡村孩子亦然。学习英语事关每个乡村孩子未来发展的可能,不仅是国际交往的未来发展的可能,更是用另一种视角认知世界的未来发展的可能,同时也事关国家人才筛选需要,事关国家深化对外开放的基本国策。所以,只要是在国家教育体系之内,乡村孩子就必须学习英语。

当然,对于如何确定各种"用"的内涵,各种"用"在各学段的要求,甚至每个学习者是否以及如何对各种"用"进行选择,以及如何学得各种"用"等等,则需要另外讨论。

记者:如何从动机角度促进农村学生的英语学习?

鲁子问:我国乡村幅员辽阔,学生也多种多样,他们有着各种不同的英语学习动机。比如,有相当一部分学生希望通过学习英语在以后能够进入高一级的学校去学习,比如从高中到大学,甚至出国学习。也有少部分学生可能希望以后能够参与更多的国际交流,尤其是在边疆地区,一些学生已经有了很多的跨境交流需要,他们更希望能够学好英语。比如,在中国与东盟教育周的活动中,我们就发现有很多这样的案例。同时,也有些学生只是因为对用英语所呈现的某些东西感兴趣,比如电影和电子游戏,他们带着这样的动机来学习英语。我们也发现还有一些别的动机,比如把自己家的农家乐开好,让更多外国人能够到自己的农家乐来消费。因此,学生的学习动机有非常不同的呈现形式。

那么如何基于学生多样的学习动机来促进学生的英语学习呢?我们现在找到了一种比较有效的方法,叫作"复合视角"。也就是说,不只是基于单一的动机去促进学生的学习,而是基于复合的学习动机来促进学生的英语学习。这当然对老师提出了更高的要求,但也恰恰能够更好地促进学生的英语学习,这才是我们更需要去努力的一个方向。

至于实践,我们这些年来做了一些尝试,取得了一些进步,也希望更多老师来关注我们的实践成果,和我们一起更好地推动我国乡村地区的英语教育,尤其是乡村贫困地区的英语教育。不要让英语教育成为制约教育公平的一个因素,而是要让英语教育成为促进教育公平的一个因素,使乡村学生也能享受高质量的英语教育。

记者:您曾提出,我国教育已经进入全面发展学生核心素养的时代,而发展核心素养的基础是课堂。乡村中学由于教学设施以及师资的匮乏,英语教学环境一直没有得到有效的改善。在这种情况下,您认为农村中学英语课堂该如何培养学生的核心素养?

鲁子问:在语言能力发展方面,乡村条件和基础远不如城市,而且语言环境等要素短期难以改变,乡村学生英语语言能力发展受到很大制约。而核心素养发展则不同,乡村学生和城市学生同步开始核心素养发展,乡村英语教育有追赶的可能。

发展学生核心素养,对于乡村英语教育,首先最应该做的是转变教师的英语教育观念,使他们尽快转换到促进学生核心素养发展的轨道上来。乡村家长对英语教育改革的干预程度大大低于城市家长,这是乡村英语教育转轨的优势。我最近调查发现,乡村教师也愿意转轨到核心素养上来。问题是:谁引导他们、帮助他们转?

这些年,我们为地方政府起草了多份方案,我们也加大了乡村教师培训的力度,推动乡村英语课堂变革。

我认为,建设促进学生核心素养发展的乡村英语课堂,首先要从课堂教育教学目标入手,以核心素养为终极目标,把英语知识学习与技能发展整合到核心素养目标中去。我们最近先从高中课堂入手,为每一单元制定了整合性的目标,发给老师参考使用,希望对此有所推动。然后是教学过程要始终指向核心素养,不能陷入繁琐的知识教学、取巧的技能教学之中。当然,最终还是必须有评价考试改革、高校招生制度改革。这方面则需要新时代评价改革政策的推进。

对于教育改革,我自己作为一线教师,会努力做好我们能做的,静待我们不能做的领域的变化。我们希望有更多部门和我们一道努力,共同推动乡村英语教育弯道发力,缩小与城市英语教育的差距,实现城乡英语教育共同发展。

记者:农村中学英语教师是农村教育改革的中流砥柱,其专业发展对农村基础教育改革有重要意义。您认为核心素养理念的提出对于农村中学英语教师专业素养发展有什么指导意义?

鲁子问:这些年我一直在乡村工作,接触了大量的乡村英语教师,深知他们的艰辛与努力。基于此,作为一名来自乡村、现在在乡村工作的一线教师,我想对乡村英语教师同行们说:

首先,我们要做一名现实的理想主义者。我们要有专业发展的远大理想,成为学生的经师、人师,帮助我们的学生实现他们的辉煌人生。但是,我们更要面对现实,要脚踏实地,不期盼明天早起我们的学生就能掌握英语。我们先从现实出发,帮助学生发展,从而实现我们自己的专业发展。正如 Charlotte 在 *Charlotte's Web* 中所说:"By helping you, I was trying to lift up my life a trifle." 比如,我告诉我们正在帮扶的一所存在诸多发展困难的高中的英语教师:咱们先弄清楚高中课标和高考试题的核心素养要求,知道我们要走到哪里去;再弄清楚学生基础与可能发展,知道我们可以帮助他们发展到哪里去;之后再来分析课文,看我们如何用课文帮助学生走到那里去。这远比首先就分析课文要更加脚踏实地。这样脚踏实地地教学,学生更有收获,教师也就有了专业成就感,也就促进了自己的专业发展。

再者,我们要小步快走、坚持不懈。教师的专业发展,不可能一步登天,一蹴而就,而需要制定阶段性计划,然后努力。阶段性计划要切实可行,远期明确,近期可行,小步子起步,持续性努力,快速度发展。比如在前一案例中,我告诉老师们,我们很难一次性分析弄懂一整套试卷,我们应该从一个可以完成的题型分析开始,如和课文比较接近的阅读,但不能只停留在阅读,而应一个月分析一个题型,这样一个学年就可以实现这一项专业发展的目标了。

最后,我们要仰望天空,要深度研读课程标准、国家相关重大政策,如深化评价改革的政策;更要把握教育的育人这一根本,不只是教给学生语言知识和技能,不只是帮助学生提高成绩,更要引导学生学习做人做事,真正实现教书育人、立德树人,这样才是真正的教师专业发展。

记者:您在一线城市、全国重点高校深耕二十余年,是享誉业界的英语教育专家,可您这些年来一直在关注农村地区的英语教育,扎根偏远村寨,请问您坚持这么做的原因是什么?

鲁子问:首先是因为我曾多次参加中国农村问题调查项目,发现乡村英语教育问题远比预想的困难,也远比预想的复杂。比如,乡村小学非专任英语教师非常普遍,这既有困难,也有优势,因为可以开展基于跨学科内容的英语教学。当我结束在加拿大的工作回国时,有机会进行选择,于是就选择了民族地区乡村教育这一具有双重难度的领域,看看是否可能做一些有益的探索。

其次是因为我出身乡村,自幼在乡村长大,是乡村哺育了我。我希望在力所能及的范围之内能反哺乡村。我发现在乡村教育与民族教育领域,我可能可以做得更多更好,作用与效益更大,帮助到更多孩子和老师。

最后是因为我个人更喜欢乡村文化、熟络而且亲切的社会、尊严优先于财富的社会认可、宁静而不喧闹的环境,虽然没有我喜爱的图书馆、美术馆、博物馆,听不到我喜爱的讲座、音乐会,但在互联网时代,这些也大多可以通过网络在乡村欣赏到。而且,我也可以不时返回城市。

所以,我自己愿意投身乡村教育与民族教育,这不是倡导大家都回到乡村和民族地区,因为人类文明发展更需要具有一定规模化、集约化的城市文明。我只是希望更多人关注乡村教育,力所能及地帮助乡村教育发展,促进乡村孩子成长。

罗少茜

罗少茜,北京师范大学外国语言文学学院英文系教授。主要研究领域为二语习得、任务型语言教学、语言测试与评价、外语教师教育。代表作包括《文学教学与思辨能力培养:课例与实践》《英语测试与评价:理论与实践》《青少年外语读写能力培养》《促进学习:二语教学中的形成性评价》《任务型语言测试中的任务难度研究》《任务型语言教学》;主持及参与的项目包括"高中英语课程标准核心素养对学生表现效果的历时研究""中学英语素养测评与诊断""义务教育英语课程标准(2022 年版)研制""中国学龄儿童脑发育队列研究"。

解决中国阅读教学中的问题不能只靠阅读分级模式

北京师范大学教授罗少茜专访

记者：您认为阅读素养与阅读能力的区别是什么？

罗少茜：首先，阅读是外语学习者习得、学习语言的主要手段之一。一般来说，一个人有能力并不一定代表他有气质。阅读能力和阅读素养也是同样的道理。阅读能力是表现出来的能读、能写，而阅读素养是气质的、内在的，包括阅读习惯和阅读体验。我们提倡阅读素养的培养，实际上就是：我们不仅要培养阅读能力强的人，而且要培养真正具有阅读素养的人，这与我们的全人教育，与我们的素养教育，都是十分密切相关的。

那么如何培养和发展英语阅读素养呢？我们要在关注阅读能力培养的同时，重视学习者的阅读习惯和阅读体验，不断促进其阅读能力的发展。阅读习惯包括阅读行为、频率和阅读量，是显性和可观察的；阅读体验指阅读的态度、兴趣和自我评价，属于阅读的情感系统，是隐性的。二者共同构成阅读品格。PIRLS（Progress in International Reading Literacy Study，国际阅读素养进展研究项目）2016 年在 "What Makes a Good Reader: International Findings" 中谈到他们的发现：外语阅读素养的发展还可以从母语阅读素养的相关研究中获得启发。针对四年级学生的国际阅读素养进展研究项目发现，优秀者往往拥有能支持读写学习的家庭环境，读写学习开始时间较早并往往有积极的阅读态度。针对八年级学生的国际学生评价项目的研究结果表明，如果学生的阅读面广，阅读参与度高，而且掌握了恰当的阅读学习策略，其阅读表现就会更好。

记者：您认为目前中国英语阅读教学中普遍存在的问题是什么？

罗少茜：关于这个问题我从课堂阅读教学和课外阅读两方面来谈。

课堂阅读教学中普遍存在的问题主要有以下几点：侧重学生阅读技能的训练，忽视对学生听、说、读、写综合语言能力的培养，忽视文本与思维之间的关系，忽视对学生批判性阅读思维能力的锻炼，忽视对学生阅读素养的培养；无法充分体现以学生为中心的教学理念，学生始终处于被动阅读者的角色，等等。

课外外语读写学习的问题有以下几点：

缺乏有效指导——许多家长并不具备足够的指导学生外语读写学习的能力；缺少动机——学生如果没有养成良好的阅读习惯，可能不愿进行外语阅读；缺少读后的及时反馈——大量的课外阅读是提高阅读能力的基本条件，读后需要相应的读写服务跟进，使学生能不限时间、不限地点并且充满兴趣地学习，同时还能获得及时反馈。

当然，目前教育市场已经出现了丰富的为外语读写提供服务的应用产品，这些产品可在移动智能设备上使用，方便学生随时学习。比如有的应用软件针对英语阅读设计了分级阅读体系，学生可以反复多次地听读并朗读分级读本，再完成阅读理解练习。这类软件大多会考虑学生阅读的动机因素，学生通过阅读可以获取积分，并利用积分购买相应的玩具装备。这种游戏式的升级阅读可以有效地吸引学生进行阅读。

我也采访过一些一线教研员，如四川的高中教研员李兴勇等，他们认为存在两个问题：

一是泛读教学虚化。大家都知道泛读的重要性，但是受传统应试的影响和出于短时功利性需求，老师们大都不愿意放手让学生进行阅读。很多老师认为让学生刷阅读题比进行泛读能更快看到效果。另外一个原因是有些老师缺乏自信。受周围同事的影响，很多老师都没有对学生进行阅读习惯的培养。他们会担心：如果我放手让学生阅读，我班成绩落后了怎么办？基于这两个原因，泛读教学口号声大，但是实际操作虚化。

二是精读教学浅层化。很多精读教学仍旧只是满足于表层信息的获取，没有进行主题意义的探究。即使有，也是老师"传递"给学生，学生关于文本的主题意义的认识很多时候没有听到多元的声音。精读教学中英语学习活动观很多时候没有体现出来。

记者：您认为国外的阅读分级模式能否解决中国阅读教学中的问题？

罗少茜：阅读教学中的问题并不见得通过单纯的阅读就能解决，更不是说，分级阅读引进来就能解决我们的阅读教学中的问题。阅读教学涉及很多方面的问题，有读物的问题，有老师的问题，有学生的问题，有环境的问题，还有很多其他的问题。所以我们不能说，分级读物就可以解决我们阅读教学中的问题。但是，我们可以用分级读物补充学生的教材，扩大学生的视野。

实际上，曾玲、赵海永和我在 2021 年所做的元分析研究发现，非分级读物对外语能力的影响远远大于分级读物；而从纳入研究数量来看，使用分级读物的研究数量远超非分级读物。Hill 2013 年发文认为，分级读物往往强调语言的合适性，多为虚构内容。我和曾玲 2017 年的研究发现，非分级读物多为非虚构，而其效应量更大，说明它的内容和语言可能更适合学习者。从这个意义上来说，我们必须重视话题广泛、多种类的阅读材料，教师应尽可能提供多种材料（包括虚构和非虚构）供学生选择。另外，从阅读的目的来看，学生如要通过阅读达到个人目标、增长知识和发展个人潜能及参与社会活动，就应多读信息类材料，如报纸、杂志、非虚构书籍等。

记者：针对新课标的要求，您认为应该如何开发真实的语言素材、利用生活化的语料激发学生学习兴趣？

罗少茜：根据新课标的要求，英语课程要培养学生成为具有中国情怀、国际视野的社会主义建设者和接班人。中国情怀、国际视野是英语学科的核心价值。陈康等 2019 年发文提出，中国情怀指应增强对中华优秀传统文化、社会主义先进文化的认同，正确认识中国特色和国际比较，自觉践行社会主义核心价值观；国际视野指应了解人类文明历史和世界发展动态，具有全球意识，以开放包容的态度看待文化多样性，积极参与跨文化交流。

新课标强调语言素材的真实性、地道性。真实性是指所读文本是学生生活中真实存在的；地道性是指语言的地道。所以，我们要选择能够让学生感同身受的材料，让他们感觉到文本中发生的事、讲的故事就是自己或周围发生的事，将语言素材与学生自己、家庭、生活、学习、同学和玩伴联系起来，这样才能激发他们的学习兴趣。

阅读的力量在于其文字对我们的世界观、人生观和价值观会产生影响。因此，选择阅读材料时我们要注意材料的内涵反映人类命运共同体和多元文化特征的素材，让学生通过英语学习来加深对祖国文化的理解，有文化身份认同感，增强爱国主义情怀，坚定文化自信。

记者：您曾提出，在英语阅读教学中可以采用"阅读圈"和"合作拼图式阅读"，这两种教学方式的区别和联系是什么？英语教师在阅读课堂中应该如何有效运用这两种教学方式？

罗少茜：阅读圈也称"文学圈"，最初被用来进行文学作品阅读分享和交流，在泛读中进行了大量实践。其具体组织形式是：学生组成 3~6 人的阅读小组，小组中每个人有明确的角色分工，每个角色代表解读文本的一种视角，小组成员带着明确的目的完成阅读，填写阅读单，并基于阅读单进行组内和组间交流，实现文本深层理解和语言学习。对阅读圈感兴趣的读者可以阅读 Daniels(2002)，罗少茜、张玉美(2020)，曾玲、罗少茜(2021)所发表的文章。

合作拼图(JIGSAW)模式又称合作学习模式，是美国社会心理学家 Aronson 通过长时间的观察与研究于 1978 年提出的。通过这个模式我们调动学生的参与意识，形成相互合作、相互信任的学习氛围；作为英语教学中常用的教学模式取得了很大的成功——它能有效激发学生的学习兴趣，培养学生运用批判性思维来解决问题、沟通讨论等重要技能。Maftei & Maftei(2011)和罗少茜、谢颖(2015)都有相关文章供大家参考。

组建学习小组、任务分配以及操作过程是：首先，组建自主、合作学习小组；其次，对难易程度不同的阅读材料进行任务分配，比如可以将一篇故事分成几个部分，让每组学生负责其中一部分；对于一篇不可分解的故事，可以让每组学生负责其中一项任务：如词汇、结构、主题等；选择几篇主题相同、难度一样或不同的故事，让每组学生负责一篇。

阅读圈一般适用于虚构、故事性文本，包括教材中的记叙文。但是在教学实践中也有老师会改良后应用。在此提醒老师们将成熟的方式进行改良时要非常慎重，要思考改良是否能达到真正的效果。合作拼图阅读模式则既适合虚构故事又适合于其他非虚构类读物。

记者：我国外语教育界一直有"精读"和"泛读"问题的讨论，您认为精读和泛

读对外语能力的整体影响分别表现在什么方面?

　　罗少茜:从字面意义来看,精读就是就一篇课文或阅读材料做细致的阅读和分析;泛读就是广泛阅读。在此我重点谈泛读。首先,我们来看 Bamford 和 Day (2004)对泛读所作的定义:泛读指学习者通过阅读大量简单的外语材料来学习语言的教学方法,它能为外语学习提供大量可理解性输入。泛读主要通过隐性学习促进语言发展;隐性学习指从语言输入中不断获得习惯性的联想知识并进行语言共现模式的内隐式学习。曾玲、赵海永、罗少茜 2021 年的研究发现,隐性学习的基础是大量输入,只有在大量输入的基础上,学习者才能在无意识的情况下,从反复接触的语言中获取语言模式并掌握语言加工技能。

　　从外语教学来看,泛读在教学法上也得到支持。Nation(2007)提出在外语教学中要对聚焦于意义的输入、聚焦于意义的输出、聚焦于语言的学习和发展流利性这四个方面给予同样的重视和时间,泛读则直接服务于聚焦于意义的输入和发展流利性这两方面。

　　我们再来看泛读对外语能力发展的影响。曾玲、赵海永、罗少茜(2021)根据过去 20 年从不同角度对泛读的影响研究,采用元分析方法整合了泛读对外语能力发展影响的相关研究,研究结果表明:无论是根据实验组-对照组还是实验前-实验后研究,泛读对外语能力的影响均达到中等效应量;调节变量分析发现影响的效应量在青少年、非分级读物、网络阅读和完全替换式泛读中更大;泛读对听力、阅读理解和写作影响的效应量大于整体语言能力。在有效促进写作能力方面,原因可能是学习者通过大量输入获得了内容知识,扩大了词汇量,同时获得了句式准确性、主谓一致性、时态、数词、词序、冠词、代词和介词的相关知识,并将这些知识进行内化并应用于写作。

　　从我们的元分析结果可以得出以下结论:无论是整体语言能力,还是在外语能力的不同方面,泛读都表现出明显的影响,此发现与其他元分析一起证明了语言能力可以通过大量可理解性输入而提高,此时学习者有机会反复接触语言模式,进行隐性学习;同时获得更多的相关知识和信息,练习阅读技巧和策略,提高自动化加工程度,发展流利性。本研究的发现进一步支持在外语教学中开展泛读,同时提出将泛读扩展到儿童,并在泛读中实践多种材料内容和阅读媒介。

　　记者:当前,各种外语类 APP 的开发为人们进行外语移动学习提供了便利,您

如何看待这些阅读 APP 的出现？您认为科技在推动英语学习发展的过程中应发挥什么样的作用？

罗少茜：上面我谈到在泛读中实践多种材料内容和阅读媒介，外语阅读 APP 亦是一种学习媒介。科技在推动英语学习发展的过程中无疑起到重要的作用，促进多元读写及多模态方式的教和学。

曾玲、赵海永和我 2021 年在做有关阅读媒介的调节效应研究的过程中，发现基于网络的数字化阅读和听读对外语能力的影响大于纸质阅读。基于网络的阅读赋予学生更多的自主性和更强的交互性，Sun(2003)研究的大学生自主构建的在线阅读材料库和蒋银健 2016 年基于微信公众平台的泛读方案就说明了这一点。Day(2015)亦认为基于网络的阅读是未来泛读的趋势。而听读包含了音频和文字两种信息输入渠道，李燕芳、董奇(2011)针对儿童听读的研究表明视听双通道比视觉单通道的信息输入可能更有效，因此这种阅读方式对儿童可能更有意义。

以互联网和数码产品为媒介的数码读写活动使学生的生活不受时间和空间的局限，电子文本与其他文本、图片、声音和视频有机结合，形成有效的视觉冲击，使学生更能感受到读写的乐趣与挑战。同时，数字环境和多种传播渠道使得学生的读写世界更加复杂，教师和家长需要帮助学生在读写资源和活动中进行选择和分类；学生在课堂上学习基本方法，交流经验和知识，在课外可以通过多种渠道体验生活，获得经验，支持课堂学习。

记者：您在阅读教学方面有丰富的理论和实践经验，您认为阅读在培养英语学科核心素养的过程中发挥着什么作用？不同学段阅读教学的主要目标是什么？

罗少茜：英语课程的目标是培养和发展学生的核心素养，阅读在培养学生英语学科核心素养的过程中发挥着重要的作用。《普通高中英语课程标准(2017 年版 2020 年修订)》提出英语教学要在一定的主题语境中，基于不同类型的语篇，在主题意义引领下通过学习理解、应用实践、迁移创新等一系列体现综合性、关联性和实践性等特点的英语活动使学生促进自身语言知识学习、语言技能发展、文化内涵理解……(教育部，2020)。由此可见，语篇是培养学生英语学科核心素养的载体。阅读教学要学生运用语言技能获取、梳理、整合语言知识和文化知识，深化对语言的理解，汲取文化精华，探究主题意义。阅读教学的过程是语言能力的发展过程，也是培养文化意识、发展思维品质和培养学生学习能力的过程。

　　不同学段有不同的教学目标,培养学生阅读流畅性是阅读教学的首要任务。小学阶段重在培养学生的阅读兴趣和阅读习惯;初中和高中阶段在阅读量上有要求。以泛读方案设计为例,学习者年龄、阅读材料内容、阅读媒介、实施时长和方式这些设计因素对泛读效果有什么调节作用? 我们如何依据这些影响来设计泛读方案? 曾玲、赵海永和我 2021 年分析了学习者年龄的调节效应,发现泛读对青少年外语能力的影响最大,成人次之,儿童最小。

　　儿童进行泛读时可能需要特别注意泛读的方式。Elley & Mangubhai(1983)在小学生中进行泛读实验时使用了默读和分享阅读两种方式,结果表明阅读方式对语言能力的影响有差异,分享阅读的效果更好。Sheu 在 2003 年的研究表明改变阅读方式之前,小学生只在阅读速度上有提高;而改变阅读方式后,学生的词汇、语法、理解和阅读速度都有显著提高。由此可见,小学生泛读时可能需要更多引导和支持;而中学生和大学生则可以以默读为主,加大泛读比重,或者多泛读,少精读。

梅德明

　　梅德明,上海外国语大学教授,博士生导师,中国外语战略研究中心学术委员会主任,国家教材委员会专家委员会委员,教育部高中英语课程标准修订组组长,教育部义务教育英语课程标准修订组组长,教育部中等职业英语课程标准研制咨询专家,中国学术英语教学研究会副会长,上海国际教育考试与境外教材评价服务中心主任,上海市教育考试命题与评价指导委员会委员。主要研究方向为语言学与应用语言学、外语教育与课程建设、国家外语政策与规划、口译理论与教学等。著有《语言学与应用语言学百科全书》《现代语言学》《现代句法学》《大中小学一条龙英语人才培养模式研究》等。

助力实现教育强国，英语教育大有可为

上海外国语大学梅德明教授专访

记者：我国提出了在 2035 年建成教育强国的目标。中国英语教育可以如何为 2035 年远景目标服务？

梅德明：党和国家提出了到 2035 年基本实现社会主义现代化的远景目标，教育信息化是实现这一远景目标的重要组成部分。中国英语教育要探索基于信息技术的英语教学新模式，发展基于互联网的英语教育服务新模式，探索信息化时代的英语教育管理新模式。

中国英语教育应充分利用智能技术以加快推动英语人才培养模式和学习方法的变革，努力开展智能校园建设，构建包含交互式的数字教学和智能学习的教育体系，推动人工智能在教学科研、管理服务、资源建设等领域的全流程应用，建立以学习者为中心的育人环境，开发和完善基于大数据的智能在线教育、科研和学习的平台。英语教育界的同仁应积极参与构建网络化、数字化、智能化、个性化、终身化的英语教育体系，建设人人可以学英语、处处可以学英语、时时可以学英语的真正意义上的开放型英语大课堂。

中国英语教育进入了以素养、质量为人才培养标准的新时代，英语教育的根本任务是立德树人，英语课程必须以德育为魂，以能力为重，以基础为先，以创新为上，有一套指向学科核心素养发展和提升的外语课程，以学生为中心、立足我国、面向世界、科学先进的教育教学计划。英语课程应帮助学生树立正确的国家观、历史观、民族观和文化观，在坚定本民族文化自信的同时，关注人类命运共同体的建设，积极、主动、包容、得体地与来自多元文化背景的人们交流与合作。

当今世界的开放和交流是不以人们的意志为转移的大趋势。我们的学生将与来自不同文化背景的人交流，他们需要坚守中国立场和核心价值观，同时需要理解不同的想法和价值观，需要跨越文化差异、观点差异、价值差异，与他人建立信任并进行合作。因此，学校必须培养学生的全球胜任力，帮助学生为走向未来世界做好准备。

中国英语教育应重点培养学生五种能力：自主学习能力、提出问题的能力、跨文化交际能力、创新思维能力以及谋划未来参与建设人类命运共同体的能力。

中国英语教育应该站在新的历史起点，聚焦新时代对英语人才培养的新需求，强化以能力为重的人才培养理念，将教育信息化作为教育系统性变革的内生变量，支撑引领教育现代化发展，推动教育理念更新、模式变革、体系重构，使我国外语教育信息化水平走在世界前列，为国际教育信息化发展提供中国智慧和中国方案。

英语课程具有重要的育人功能，旨在发展学生的语言能力、文化意识、思维品质和学习能力等英语学科核心素养，落实立德树人根本任务。我们要注重在发展学生英语语言运用能力的过程中，帮助他们学习、理解和鉴赏中外优秀文化，培育中国情怀，拓展国际视野，增进国际理解，逐步提升跨文化沟通能力、思辨能力、学习能力和创新能力，形成正确的世界观、人生观和价值观。

站在历史新起点的英语教育工作者应该以发展的眼光和瞄准国际一流的质量定位，继承和发展正确的育人理念和行之有效的育人方法要求，体现外语教育的发展趋势；同时着力解决学科教育教学中存在的突出问题以及与学生发展不相适应的观念和做法。

记者：我国英语教育有哪些经验可以和世界其他国家和地区分享？

我国正在经历全球最大的信息化基础设施升级改造和师生信息素养提升培训，知识获取方式和传授方式、教和学的关系正在发生明显变化，教学理念、结构、模式、过程、方法与技术等正在发生整体性范式转变。现代信息技术与教学过程的深度融合是实现课堂革命的主要手段和必经路径。已经出现的变化包括时空开放与虚拟化、学习空间重构、教学活动回放、教学流程再造、资源供给丰富多元，等等。

多年难以实现的教学范式如先学后教、以学定教、少教多学，体验式、沉浸式、主题化、情景化、项目化、问题化和研究性的学习方式，以及"教学评"一致性和一体化的理念,这些都在逐渐转化为现实,出现在我们眼前。

我们应该正确认识新时代的数字化"课堂与世界",正确认识数字化时代的"教与学"。我认为,数字化时代的课堂只是我们教育教学的小世界,数字化时代的世界才是我们教育教学的大课堂。我们不仅要"一切为了学习者而教",我们更应该"为了一切学习者而教""为了学习者的一切而教"。数字化时代的网络资源丰富多样,大大拓展了学生的知识面,增加了学生的知识量,增强了学生学习的选择性和自由度。同时,网络资源的开放性、多元性、即时性,解构了传统教学中知识的系统性、连续性、线性化、结构化,有利于知识的组织和再组织,从单一物理环境发展为物理世界、数字世界和虚拟世界相互交融的线上线下混合学习环境。对于数字一代学习者来说,课程学习不再局限于课堂。全方位的移动学习,如校内学习、家庭学习、社区学习、场馆学习、游戏学习,确保了我们的学习无时不在,学习无处不在。

新时代的数字学习环境是一种基于信息化思维模式、运用现代教育技术而创建的智能化模式的多元学习环境。这种学习环境对学习者提出诸多主动性要求:主动感知信息,主动加工数据,主动建构知识,主动交流体验。

我们应该重新定义新时代的学习空间。新时代的学习模式应该是线上学习+线下学习的混合学习模式,是主动学习、合作学习、互动学习、探究学习的 2.0 版。数字教育技术如 AR(增强现实)、VR(虚拟现实)和 MR(混合现实)可以同步创造内容生动有趣、参与度高的沉浸式课程,从而提高教学效果。外语课堂使用 VR 虚拟现实技术,能够将外部世界带到教室,也能将教室带到外面,而学生通过 Cospaces,能够与全世界分享自己的虚拟创造。在 VR 中,我们可以身临其境地体验世界。在 AR 中,我们可以看到虚实融合的新世界,在全息环境下接受教育。学生在智慧空间与他人和他物连接和交流,得到沉浸式、交互式、自动化的体验。现代化教室应该为学生创设有利于合作的空间,促进学生的合作学习。科技的引进有助于创立新型学习空间。21 世纪的课堂使用的是智能板,教室里摆放的是智能课桌,课堂上学生进行虚拟的户外考察和交际活动,而非单纯读课文。在此过程中,学生也在创造媒介,而非仅仅是被动地观看视频。

记者:中国英语教育在构建"人类命运共同体"中需要承担何种责任和使命?这将对我国英语教育产生何种影响?

梅德明:"人类命运共同体"是我们国家提出的一个重要的全球价值观。习主席多次提出，我们要有"人类命运共同体"意识，要努力构建人类命运共同体，这对我们的学科教育，尤其是外语学科，非常重要。这个世界，不管你愿意不愿意，都是一个整体。我们身处这个世界，不仅要关注当地的问题，更要关注全球问题、跨地区和跨文化的问题。这个世界是互联的，一定也是互助的，同时也应该互鉴，所以"互联互助互鉴"是我们教育工作者在体现人类命运共同体的理念、构建人类命运共同体整个实施的过程中必须具有的大观念。我们要为国家的富强、民族的复兴做出我们应有的努力。同时，我们应该在一个更大的、全球的视野下看到很多地区问题，也都可能是全球问题。很多地区问题的解决，可能要从全球的视野去考虑，用全球的观念、全球的方法去处理。

那么我们外语学科在回答"培养什么人""如何培养人"和"为谁培养人"的三个重大问题上，要从构建人类命运共同体的历史使命，要从赋予我们学生这种跨文化交流与合作的能力，文明对话、文明互鉴的这种方法上以及我们"心系天下"的中华情怀上回答。因此，我们课程的理念、课程的目标、课程的内容、课程的方法、课程的实施以及课程的评价都要渗透"人类命运共同体"的意识和观念，都要助力构建"人类命运共同体"这一伟大事业。

也就是说，我们必须明白，我们所培养的学生未来是进入世界的。这是一个非常不确定的世界，一个很不稳定的世界。但是我们有了中国情怀、国际视野、跨文化沟通能力，就有了自己的定力。只要我们定位准确，虽然前进的道路上可能有很多艰难险阻，但是我们给予孩子的这种价值观和胜任力将使他们终身受益，最终也会成就我们伟大祖国复兴的伟业。所以我们在这里通过我们举办的大会，也通过我们的新闻媒体，主动解读我们新研制的英语课程标准，介绍我们在外语教育、英语学科发展方面确立的新理念，把语言能力、文化意识、思维品质和学习能力这几个学科核心素养的综合发展视为新课程建设的大方向，以素养立意，使立德树人在英语课程中有效落地，就是出于这个目标。我相信我们这个理念一定会得到越来越多的一线教师和学生的呼应，因为这个理念是以学生的未来为考量的，也是以祖国和世界的未来为出发点的。我们大家共同努力，一定会把这个工作落到实处。而且我们已经见到了很多非常成功的教学案例，我们的孩子也越来越多地关心祖国，关心世界，关心未来，关心他们的终身发展，包括发展跨文化交流与合作的能力。

记者：谈到英语教育的具体实践，您认为培养学生的英语阅读素养应该注重哪些方面？

梅德明：培养英语阅读素养对我们的孩子来说，不应该停留在词汇和语法层面，更应该进入意义层面，进入语篇、语篇的主题意义、语篇的育人功能、语篇作者和语篇学习者之间的关系。要学会思辨。阅读其实是一种积极思维活动，在阅读过程中，尤其是读后反思过程中，我们不仅培养了语言能力、文化意识和学习策略，更提升了思维品质，尤其是提升了思维在逻辑性、创造性和批判性方面的品质。我认为有效的阅读应该体现这三个方面的要求。

记者：针对新课标的要求，您认为应该如何开发真实的语言素材，利用生活化的语料激发学生的学习兴趣？

梅德明：我们开发教材或者学习材料，应结合现实的社会情景和生活情景。我们对资源的开发需要更加努力，报刊、杂志这一类载体跟社会生活紧密相关，应该是我们获取信息的主要渠道之一。我们也应该关注在学习过程中，能够用我们所学的外语讲述中国故事。需要能够帮助我们讲好中国故事、宣传中华文化的语篇和教材。我认为我们的阅读量还很不够，远远不能满足我们孩子成长的需求，有限的语言输入无法促进有效的语言输出。如果说我们真的能够让阅读在促进语言能力、文化意识、思维品质和学习能力的发展过程中起到应有的作用，现在的阅读要翻倍，尤其是课外阅读。要选择编辑得非常好的读物。有些分级读物非常经典，也有些分级读物跟社会生活相关，所以我们应该把关注力聚焦于一切可以为我所用的阅读资源上。当然，我们会碰到各种各样的困难。但是，阅读就是心智成长，阅读就是人的发展，阅读就是与世界互动，这样的理念在任何时候都不会过时。

记者：您曾说过英语教育不仅仅是关于语言的教学，还在于培养学生多方面的能力。但是现在依然有很多人认为语言只是一个工具。您对这个观点怎么看？

梅德明：我认为这个观点有很大的问题。语言是工具，但这仅仅是整个问题的一小部分。语言体现的是人、人的心智活动、概念的形成、意义的表达、思想的交流，语言就应该发挥这样的作用。我们不会否认语言作为一种工具，我们也认为语言应该成为我们的交流工具，我们要把这个工具学好用好。但是我们也要看到，语言学习的背后是文化学习、思维发展以及跨文化交流能力的形成。

语言到底是什么？人到底是什么？人和语言到底是什么关系？语言成为我们

身心的一部分，它不仅仅是我们的"嘴"、我们的"手"、我们的"眼睛"、我们的"耳朵"，它更是我们的"大脑"和"心灵"。因为语言要靠思维、要靠概念、要靠理念、要靠观点、要靠想法统整起来，因此对于外语教育，以及母语教育，我们都应该贯彻一种全人培养的理念，不能把它仅仅是看作一个工具，因为如果说语言或者外语仅仅是一个工具，那么这个工具很快就会被人工智能替代。现在我们已经看到了人工智能在语言服务方面所取得的成长和进步。我们应该关注得更多的是我们的软实力、我们的隐性能力。也就是说，在我们进行理性教育的时候，我们的感性教育，我们的情感教育，我们的审美教育，我们的文化观、历史观、国家观、未来观，都应该通过我们的大脑和心灵，通过我们思维的碰撞，通过我们理念的不断呈现，通过我们人与人之间的交流，形成共同的想法来推动。人之所以为人，言也；人之所以为人，思也。言为心声，思以言表。妙道之言，直指人心；妙言之道，尽得风流。真可谓"此中有真意，欲辨已忘言"。因此，这是一个方向盘与方向盘操控者之间的关系，航船和航道之间的关系。

束定芳

　　束定芳，上海外国语大学教授，博士生导师，上海市英语教育教学研究基地首席专家，《外国语》杂志主编，中国英汉语比较研究会认知语言学专业委员会会长，*Cognitive Linguistic* 等国际期刊编委，国际认知语言学研究会常务理事（2015—2017）。2001 年获"上海市曙光学者"称号；2006 年入选教育部"新世纪人才"计划；2009 年获"上海市领军人才"称号；2017 年入选中宣部"文化名家暨'四个一批'"人才计划和国家第三批"万人计划"（哲学社会科学领军人才）。曾获国家基础教育课程改革教学研究成果二等奖（2010）、教育部哲学社会科学优秀研究成果奖（2011）、全国百篇优秀博士论文指导教师奖（2012）、高等教育国家级教学成果二等奖（2014）等。

重新认识中小学外语教育的意义与方法

上海外国语大学束定芳教授专访

记者：中国为什么要把外语作为中小学的一门重要的基础课程？

束定芳：我们知道，语言能力是人类区别于其他动物的标志性特征。人类的儿童一出生就具备了在社会环境中自动习得一门或多门语言的能力。学习语言的过程实际上就是儿童社会化的过程，是其融入本语言社团，接受其社会规范、价值观念和文化传统的过程。一方面，语言的词汇和结构中凝聚着大量的本语言社团历史发展的信息和文化价值取向，掌握语言就意味着同时获得了有关本语言社团的相关知识和文化信息；另一方面，人们通过语言与他人交流，认知周围的世界，获取更多的知识和文化信息。所以，语言是一个人在社会生存和发展的工具。语言能力是一个人学习能力的体现，也是综合素养的体现。

如果一个人学习并掌握一门外语，这就意味着他可以通过这门额外的语言来学习用这种语言记录和书写的历史文化和科学知识。外语学习拓展了学习者交流的范围和学习的能力，使他可以获得更多的生存和发展的资源。世界正处在一个全球化的时代，在母语之外，再掌握一门或多门其他重要的语言，对一个人的发展至关重要。在美国教育界，甚至有人喊出了"只懂一种语言是 21 世纪的文盲"的口号，获得了广泛认同。

外语能力也是一个国家发展的重要资源。中国的发展离不开改革开放，改革开放离不开懂外语的各类人才。因此，在基础教育阶段培养学生的外语能力不仅仅是为学生成长和发展服务，也是国家改革开放、面向未来持续发展的一项重要国策。其实,中国越发展,文明水平越高,外语能力越重要。随着中国越来越多地参与国际事务和全球治理,不仅仅需要懂一种外语或者只懂英语的人才,还需要懂多种外语的人才。

记者:"双减"背景下,中小学生如何学习外语最有效?

束定芳:根据学术界最新的研究成果,儿童是在使用语言的过程中掌握语言的。儿童使用语言是为了与周围的人互动,而不是学习语言本身。儿童是在与他人互动中、在探索周围的世界过程中不知不觉地学会了语言。语言成为儿童成长和学习、与社会交流的一个工具和载体。其实,在一定的年龄段,特别是在青春期之前,只要有适当的语言环境,儿童同时学会两三门语言也是不太费力的事情。当然,说"不太费力"实际上是他们没有意识到需要"用力",因为他们的注意力集中在通过学习和使用语言达到其他的目的上。

学习外语的目的是能够使用外语。因此,学习外语的最好方法,也与母语学习一样,是通过使用这门语言掌握该语言。当然这种使用与母语习得有所区别。儿童掌握母语是个不知不觉的过程,因为他/她学母语的过程也是他/她认知周围世界的过程。他/她不但用自己的感知器官去认知周围的世界,还通过语言交流来观察和理解周围的世界。因此,语言是手段,不是目的。外语学习则是在母语能力的基础上,在一个缺乏自然的语言环境的情况下学习的。外语既是目的,也是手段之一。因此,如何利用学生的母语能力和认知能力来帮助他们逐步获得外语能力,如何帮助学生在"使用外语"学习其他知识、探索世界的过程中"不知不觉"地掌握外语,是一个需要不断探索和适应的过程。

由于大部分学生不可能长时间接触外语作为母语的人或老师,因此,学校的环境、外语教师的语言能力、课堂教学的方法就特别重要。外语课堂上,外语教师要尽量用外语与学生交流,交流学生感兴趣的话题,帮助学生通过外语学习了解周围的世界,或者学习新的知识,而不是仅仅通过教语法、背词汇、通过做练习题特别是语法练习题来教学生。后者不但事倍功半,而且因为这样的外语学习枯燥无味,很容易使学生失去学习的兴趣,形成心理负担,影响其健康成长,得不偿失。

另外,根据国内外学者的观察和研究,学习一门外语,只要学习者目标明确,学习得法,肯下功夫,在任何阶段都有可能成功。早在 20 多年前,我们就提出了"适当推迟、集中学习、强化训练、专业提高"的十六字外语教学改革方针。在没有高质量的外语师资的情况下,小学外语课程可以晚一点开设。已经开设的,特别是在一二年级就开设外语的学校,也没有必要取消,因为早学也有早学的好处,毕竟现在外语学习的条件和资源比20年前好了很多,师资队伍情况也大为改善。

"双减"其实为基础外语教育改革提供了一个契机。小学外语教学的目的不是把语言作为一门学科知识,让学生去学习语法或者词汇本身,而是通过(让学生)接触外语,在使用外语的过程中培养学生对外语的兴趣,初步了解外语与母语的不同,初步了解一些有关的目标语文化和世界其他国家和地区文化,逐步培养学生的语言能力;(让学生)通过学习和阅读与其外语能力匹配的外语材料接触世界文化,使其体验由外语学习获得新知识、开阔视野的乐趣,因而愿意自己去进行更多的课外阅读或接触更多的多模态语言材料,提升自己的综合素养。

就中国特殊的外语学习环境、教育体制和师资条件以及学习者的认知能力发展情况而言,初中和高中阶段实际上都是外语学习的最佳时机。学生学习的成效在很大程度上取决于学校和教师的引导。外语课堂教学的目标是培养学生使用语言的能力,课堂是师生使用外语交流思想、通过外语拓展知识、进行文化比较和思维训练的场所,在语言使用中提高使用语言的能力。初中阶段的外语学习应该侧重培养学生的阅读能力,使其能够直接阅读原版图书,具备一定的口头和书面交流能力;高中阶段可以培养综合使用语言的能力,特别是公共演讲和写作能力。当然,这不是说,课堂教学中不能学习语言知识本身,包括语法知识和词汇知识。实际上,在适当的时机,在学生对语言使用有一定的感性认识的基础上,适当地帮助学生发现和总结语法规则和词汇使用知识,能够起到举一反三、事半功倍的效果。

因此,在"双减"背景下,如何在有限的课堂教学时间内组织学生通过使用外语而获得外语能力,同时培养学生的学习能力,鼓励学生通过课外阅读,汲取学科知识或百科知识,在使用外语的过程中提升语言能力、综合素养和思维能力,这需要外语教师和教研部门根据实际情况进行探索和试点。一方面,教师培训中应该把提升教师的语言使用能力作为一个重点。教师语言能力提升了,他(她)在课堂上与学生用外语互动的时间和质量提升了,学生的外语水平就会水涨船高;教师的语言能力越强,教学的目的越明确,学生学习的效果就越好;另一方面,教育管理部门要通过新课标、新教材的实施与培训,帮助教师尽快更新教学的理念和方法。

记者：如何理解外语学习过程中的测评？

束定芳：外语教学过程中，测评不可避免。学生的学习成效需要通过一定的方式来跟进考核，无论是考试还是考查。但测评应该与学习的目标一致，即关注学生语言使用的能力，而不是语言知识本身。因此，如何协调好教、学、评之间的关系，以评促学，"学、教、评"一体化，是"双减"背景下外语教育研究者、教师和管理部门的另一个重要课题。

记者：上海的英语教育在课程设计、教材开发方面有哪些值得向全国推介的经验？

束定芳：从 20 世纪 90 年代末开始，上海基础教育界经历了两期改革。从二期课改开始，上海有一个非常好的做法，就是根据上海的实际情况，制定自己的课程标准，编写自己的教材。很多骨干教师，包括教研员和特级教师，参与了教材编写，这对他们的专业发展非常重要。因为要编课标、编教材，他们就必须对国家的教育政策、国际的发展趋势和上海的实际情况有所了解，所以这个过程对他们来讲，是一个专业发展的非常好的契机。同时，教材编好以后，他们参与对其他一线教师的培训，对新教材的使用、新理念和新方法的推广都有非常大的作用，因为这些老师可以去跟一线的老师宣讲教材的特色，宣讲新的理念。

《普通高中英语课程标准（2017 年版，2020 年修订）》颁布后，上海也组织了新教材的编写，这是由上海市英语教学研究基地来主持的。上海共有两套英语教材，既有大学的学者参与编写，也有大量的中学骨干教师参与。同样，这些老师在编写过程中要对课标做深入的了解，还要学习国外教材编写的经验，所以，他们对课标的理解和对新的教学要求的了解比那些没有参与过的老师要深刻得多。教材编好以后，他们就成为教师培训、新教材使用培训的骨干力量。所以，我们很多相关的新教材使用的一些项目，他们都参与了。另外，我觉得上海市教委教研室、上海市教委基教处在新教材的编写和使用过程当中，都有非常好的想法，组织工作也做得非常好。比如，新教材开始使用以后，教研室每月有一次全市范围的教研活动，会有一位优秀教师来演绎怎么使用新教材，大家一起观摩；同时还有专家做针对性的学术讲座和点评。上海在教材编写、促进教师发展、新教材使用、促进课堂教学改革方面非常值得其他地区学习。

王守仁

　　王守仁,南京大学人文社会科学资深教授,博士生导师。曾任教育部高等学校大学外语教学指导委员会主任委员、中国外国文学学会副会长、英语文学研究分会会长。主要研究方向为英美文学和英语教育。主持并完成多项国家级重点重大研究项目。由其主持的"高素质外语人才跨文化能力培养体系创新与实践"获国家级教学成果一等奖。曾获首届国家级教学名师奖、"宝钢教育优秀教师"特等奖、全国杰出教学奖、"全国教材建设先进个人"等荣誉称号。

面向世界的中国英语教育

——从我的英语学习经验谈起

南京大学王守仁教授专访

记者：中国学习英语的人数众多，如何有效地学习英语是全社会关注的焦点。作为英语教育专家，您能否分享一些学习英语的成功经验？

王守仁：有效学习是个很好的问题。上海交通大学杨惠中教授提出过"有效教学、有效测试"的观点。Learning 是从学习者角度提出问题。中国英语教学存在"费时低效"的问题，有其客观原因。英语是外语，学习者基本上是一走出教室，就处于汉语世界，不用英语进行交际，没有使用英语的环境。所谓"费时"，是指持续时间长，从小学一年级一直到博士都在学英语。实际上无论是在基础教育还是高等教育阶段，英语课程在总课时中占比很低，学生每学期学习英语的时间并不多，但战线拖得太长。

我本科读的是英语专业，一二年级时花大力气进行听说读写的强化训练，大量阅读——精读、泛读，坚持天天听广播，大声朗读，勤于动笔，写出正确的句子和段落。总而言之，那时打下了扎实的语言基础，受益终身。多年前外研社出版的《英语门槛有多高》收录了我的一篇短文"利用一切机会接触英语"，我在文中分享了学习英语的成功经验。我提出要避免"三天打鱼，两天晒网"，持之以恒，必有收获。再具体一点，要挑选一本高质量教材，认认真真地学习，做完全部练习，掌握精读、略读、寻读、批判性阅读等阅读技能。

每个人对英语水平的要求不同。我在英国读硕士和博士时，需要大量阅读，上

50

课要参与讨论交流,最重要的是要写出学位论文。在高校任教需要写英文论文在国外期刊发表,都属于学术性写作,需要专门训练。公务员或商务人士也会出于不同需要使用英语。因此,使用导向是促进语言水平提高的动力。

记者:在全球化背景下,英语已成为商业、教育、传媒等许多领域的通用语。然而,有些人认为英语学习被过分重视了,可能会对中国文化产生不良影响,妨碍我们对母语的学习。您对此有何看法?

王守仁:母语学习与外语学习是相互促进的关系。欧洲人能说多种语言是常态。我曾有意识地观察幼儿学习英语的情况,发现儿童在语言习得阶段,只是多记了几个音符,例如苹果这一水果可以用中文说,也可以说 apple,对他们并无负担,交替使用,切换自然,还增加乐趣。学术大师如钱锺书、季羡林等,他们外语好,中文也是一流,外语并不影响他们的汉语,所谓英语冲击语文,经不起推敲。

2013 年北京市教委发布《高考改革框架方案》,提出对英语科目的分值进行大幅度调整,实行社会化考试。一石激起千层浪。有一段时间社会舆论对英语教育"进行了一场围攻"。网络社交媒体出现了一些缺乏科学依据的偏激观点,如将语文水平的下降归咎于英语学习,称英语教育"祸国殃民",是"卖国教育"。这些情绪化、极端民族主义的言论在公众中造成了思想认识上的混乱,对我国英语教育产生了消极影响。2014 年 9 月《国务院关于深化考试招生制度改革的实施意见》公布,确认"保持统一高考的语文、数学、外语科目不变,分值不变",无端指责英语教育的舆论开始平息下来。

语文教育本身存在问题,需要改进,而不应该"甩锅"给英语。英语是当今世界经济、政治、科技、文化等活动中广泛使用的语言,其地位是历史形成的,没有其他语言可以替代,全世界非英语国家也都使用英语进行交流。如教育部召开在线教育研讨会,俄罗斯、罗马尼亚、突尼斯、摩洛哥等国家学者参加交流,大家都使用英语。如果使用母语,就需要配备专门翻译,给交流带来不便。

现在机器翻译发展势头很好,是否可以依靠机器翻译而不学英语?客观地讲,人工智能在翻译领域尚处于起步阶段,机器翻译需要语料库建设,而各人的需求不一样,难以定制满足。机器翻译常常出现很多翻译错误/笑话;机器翻译还需要确认。如果自己不懂原文,就不知道机器翻译是否准确。即使有机器翻译,也需自己懂英语,才可以很自然地直接交流,而将机器作为辅助。

学习外语的功用在于让国人"睁眼看世界",可以直接接触国外的信息。翻译总是有筛选,有滞后,自己掌握了工具,就可以消除这个环节。学习语言,更大的价值是树立全球视野,了解世界。设想如果 19 世纪中叶中国老百姓都懂英语,知道英国在搞工业革命,我们国家就不会那么落后、挨打了。近代中国经历了从自以为是"天下"的中心到把自己放在"世界"一员位置上的转变,外语帮助我们了解外部世界在发生什么,形成一种开放的心胸。过去是学习外国,现在同时还要传播中国文化,更需要英语。因此,英语对于中国的发展、实现中国梦都十分重要。我们不是要弱化英语教育,而是要改进英语教育。

记者:您曾提到,中国要融入国际社会,消除语言障碍和打破贸易壁垒同等重要。您能否再详细解释一下?

王守仁:在 2017 年"一带一路"国际合作高峰论坛开幕式上,习近平主席说:"国之交在于民相亲,民相亲在于心相通。"语言互通是促进人民交往的桥梁和纽带。在当前世界大变局的形势下,如何让中国融入国际社会,面临许多挑战。

现在出现的一系列逆全球化现象表明,仅有好的产品、好的技术是不够的,如果对方因为偏见、无知、误解、敌意而抵制产品,我们的东西再好也卖不出去。国际贸易、国际政治、全球治理非常复杂,受多种因素特别是意识形态的影响,掌握外语具有现实意义。语言不仅仅应技能熟练,而且是要提升到话语层面,与对方的历史、文化、理念、价值观、表达方式等全方位互文对接,实现有效交际。

中国融入国际社会,无论是阐释中国立场、讲好中国故事,还是参与制定国际规则、提升国际话语权、保护国家利益,都需要我们的专业人员有非常高的语言水平。我们还缺乏高端语言人才,能口若悬河、能辩论、能抗争、能说服别人的国际化人才不多,而这是国家急需的。打贸易战是通过谈判,打官司处理纠纷也要通过说和写。如果外语语言能力弱,会处于十分不利的位置。

记者:您在高校从事教学和研究已三十多年,您认为英语语言教学是否应被国内高等院校纳入通识教育,而不仅仅是必修课程? 大学英语教育对学生的发展有什么实践意义和长期影响?

王守仁:我担任了两届教育部高等学校大学外语教学指导委员会主任委员(2006—2017),致力于推进大学生接受良好的外语教育,首先是英语,同时包括德语、法语、俄语等语种。高校可根据需要和师资条件开设相应课程,如同济大学的大学的德语教学就有悠久的传统。我个人的主张是,大学生要学习英语,要以积极的态度发展多语种大学外语教学,开设除英语外的第二、第三外语课程。从国家层面看,今天高校的莘莘学子正是明天社会主义建设事业的生力军。许国璋先生在回答"语言是什么"的问题时说,他比较喜欢"语言是一种社会力量"这一提法,而"语言的力量只是在各行各业有所精专的人身上充分发挥"。在 21 世纪,中国的对外开放范围更大,领域更广,层次更高,我们需要切实提高"各行各业有所精专的人"的英语水平,迎接未来社会挑战,而大学英语的使命和担当就是让未来的科学家、工程师、经济学家、法律专家、人文学科专家学者掌握外语这个斗争武器。从个人发展来讲,学习英语是为未来打基础。我国高校研究生教育发展迅速,攻读研究生学位、从事科学研究,学习英语是必需的。还有相当一部分学生直接就业,随着国际化进程的推进,懂英语是加分的。另外,不能单从是否有用来决定学什么,培训与教育是有区别的,外语教育对人的知识结构、思维方式、比较视角等都会产生深远影响。

记者:您前面提到,应花力气建设和发展英语学科,同时促进英语在现实生活中的使用。您也提出,学术英语课程不应取代大学通用英语课程。您能为我们解释一下吗?

王守仁:这是两个不同概念:一个是英语专业建设,另一个是大学英语教学。专业建设也指学科建设,主要任务是提高英语语言文学的研究水平和人才培养质量。2017 年,教育部正式启动"双一流"(一流大学和一流学科)建设,北京大学、北京外国语大学、上海外国语大学、南京大学的外国语言文学学科入选一流学科建设名单,其中包括英语语言文学学科建设。中国建设一流英语学科,应当符合新时期我国高等教育的要求,即中国特色、世界水平、时代特征。我们倡导立足中国、面向世界、人才培养与学术研究并重、研究外国与关注中国并重、国际化与本土化并重。"扎根中国大地办大学",在中国语境下办外语专业,最显著的特点、不可替代性应该是"跨文化"。我们的外语专业不同于欧美国家的母语专业,因为我们是为中国的社会主义建设培养人才。中国的一流外语人才应该具有跨文化这一关键能力和必备素养,连接中外,双向融通。

关于非外语专业的大学英语教学中通用英语与学术英语的关系,有人提出大学英语的教学定位"必须修正为专门用途英语教学定位"。通用英语并不等于基础英语,听说读写译等语言技能有不同层次要求,如英语演讲、辩论、写作等,难度相当大。即使是阅读,英语原著文本因其内容的深刻性、语法结构的复杂性以及词汇的丰富性,在语言和认知两个层面会造成理解障碍。必须看到,大部分高中毕业生的英语实际水平是相当低的。进入大学后,他们的英语能力还需进一步提高,对于大部分大学新生而言,在通用英语方面有非常大的提升空间。专门用途英语是以增强学生运用英语进行学术和职场交流为目的,具体包括学术英语(通用学术英语、专门学术英语)和职场英语两类课程。其实,从语言能力来看,通用英语与专门用途英语并不是对立关系。《欧洲语言共同参考框架:学习、教学、评估》(*Common European Framework of Reference for Languages: Learning, Teaching and Assessment*)在其对语言能力量表的描述中,达到 B2 至 C2 的语言中高级水平者可以用该语言进行专业的学习和研究:B2 的学习者能够理解"专业领域的技术性讨论课题";C1 的学习者"在其社会、职业或学术生活中,能有效、灵活应用语言"。专门用途英语中的学术英语和职场英语相对而言是目前大学英语教学的"短板",因此各高校要加强专门用途英语课程建设,开展学术英语教学研究。

但是,通用英语也应该是教学重点。如中国人民大学从培养具有跨文化沟通能力的国际化人才需要出发,强化英语口语和写作教学,自主开发实施中国人民大学英语口语能力和写作能力标准及测试。大学外语教学要注重培养国际化领导人素质,使我们的学生具有国际视野、跨文化领导力,能运用"语言的力量"去说服人、引领团队;能讲好中国故事,传播好中国声音,表达好中国观点。如果定位单一的学术英语教学,只学计算机英语、化学英语、工程英语等,是按"工具人"的培养规格要求,忽略了跨文化领导力的培养,不符合国家发展的战略需求。

另外,大学本科教育为学生提供基础性教育,学生未来发展去向多元,特别是我国高等教育进入大众化阶段后,相当一部分本科生毕业后从事的工作与所学专业无关,单一的学术英语教学并不能真正实现"学以致用"之目的。我国高等教育分为本科和研究生两个层次,本科教育并不代表高等教育全部。大学英语作为公共基础课,通常在本科一二年级开设,学生刚进校园不久,尚未进入专业学习。学术英语应该是研究生层次的核心学习内容,不必要求许多刚入校的本科新生过早学习。

记者：您认为中国大学英语教育的主要目标是什么？该如何实现呢？

王守仁：就非英语专业学生学习的大学英语教学而言，是要提高其英语运用能力，一方面是一般社会场合的交流能力，能够用英语准确、得体地表达自己的思想和感情，参与一般性议题的讨论和辩论，讲述自己和中国的故事，必要时驳斥国外某些偏见和谎言，让世界听到中国的声音；另一方面是在专业场合能够用英语进行学术交流，自然科学、社会科学和人文学科专业的学生学习用英语读论文、写论文。教育部关于大学外语教学改革提出了"一精多会""一专多能"的理念，要求培养精通一门外语、会用多门外语沟通交流、掌握一种专业、具有多种外语能力的复合型人才。"一精"主要是指英语，而多种外语能力中英语能力也是最主要的。通过实施改革，使我们的学生专业出色，外语优秀。

记者：在过去二十年中，各种新技术在语言教学中得以广泛运用，如计算机、移动应用程序和人工智能。您对英语语言教学中的科技有何看法？您认为科技在推动英语学习中应扮演什么角色？

王守仁：我一直倡导使用信息技术，在十多年前就写文章提出"把网络信息技术与外语课程整合"的理念。在信息技术与互联网发展日新月异的今天，"互联网+"深刻影响着我们的生活习惯、思维方式、经济模式等，促使知识学习、获得、产生的方式发生变化，给高等教育带来冲击、挑战和机遇。"互联网+教育"的一项重要发展成果是大规模在线开放课程（即慕课）等新型在线开放课程在世界范围的迅速兴起。在线开放课程的产生、发展和应用，对高等教育教学改革产生了深刻影响，已经开始突破现有的教学模式，促进教学方式方法和学习方式朝着教学方式混合化、教学资源开放化、学生学习个性化、学习过程社会化的方向转变。

在教育部的政策引导下，中国英语教育工作者积极探索，不断提高使用信息技术的意识和能力，在课堂教学设计与实施过程中融入并合理使用信息技术元素。就慕课建设而言，北京外国语大学联合其他高校搭建了"中国高校外语慕课平台"；清华大学、吉林大学、哈尔滨工业大学、国防科学技术大学、北京科技大学等制作的大学英语慕课在"爱课程""学堂在线"等平台上线；有的学校充分利用网上优质教育资源，安排学生选修 edX、Coursera 等国际慕课平台上授课语言为英文的慕课作为大学英语学习内容。网络空间将永久性地改变我们的高等教育，赋予英语教育新的形态。

记者：您在南京大学任教，也因研究而闻名，成为一名好老师和出色的学者，您是怎样兼顾这两个角色的？

王守仁：我目前担任南京大学教师教学发展中心主任，中心的主要任务是提升教师的教学能力。就教师发展而言，1991 年美国教育联合会发表标题为《大学教师发展：国力的提升》的报告书，对教师发展提出了经典的界定，认为大学教师发展应该包括五个方面，即：专业发展、教学发展、个人发展、课程发展和组织发展。可见，教学发展只是教师发展的一个维度。专业发展或学术发展旨在提高教师学术水平，使其创造新知识，跟踪学科前沿。高校许多外语教师的专业发展不理想，结果影响了整体的教师发展。

我个人认为，要成为一个称职的高校老师，应在五个维度同时并进。高校外语教师必须强化专业发展，这对个人及学科都具有重要意义。首先要转变观念，树立专业发展意识。不少外语教师把自己看成是教书的，而不是做学问的，把主要时间和精力都放在上课上，平时无暇阅读学术著作和学术文章，跟踪学科前沿也就无从谈起。与其他学科致力于著书立说的教师相比，在现行考评机制下，以教学为主业的外语教师忙于备课、上课，少做或不做研究，自然处于不利地位。学术研究的本质是在现有知识体系的基础上创造新知识，需要孜孜不倦地探究未知领域，分析国家发展和社会进步的需求，发现和设计新的选题，选择新的研究范式和方法。外语教师要把兴趣点从知识的传授转移到知识的创造，树立教研并进的观念，实现从教学为主型教师到学者型教师的转变。其实，教学发展与专业发展并不冲突，也不是零和关系，而是相互支撑和促进。

我在教学方面投入很多，获得过国家级教学成果一等奖，主讲的课程入选国家精品课程，并且制作了"英国小说"慕课，受到学习者广泛好评。同时，我对学术研究也非常重视，在 19 世纪英国文学、当代外国文学、外国文学史和现实主义研究领域都取得了丰硕的成果，承担国家社科重大项目，用中英文写作，在国内外发表专著和论文。学术研究方面的成果又反哺教学，得以开展研究性教学。我个人的经验说明，树立成为一个好老师和出色的学者的目标，可以使教师发展的道路越走越宽广而不是越走越窄。

记者：中国高校英语教师需要开展大量的研究、发表论文，才能在职业生涯中得以更好地发展。您认为对中小学教师也提出研究和论文发表的期望是否现实？

王守仁：高校与中小学的共同之处是都要向学生传授知识，但高校还要创造知识。高等教育课程内容是以高深知识为支撑、高阶思维为导向，体现专业的本质和特性，反映学科的基本问题，表达学术的核心概念和范畴，不仅仅满足于信息传递和知识引导，还要帮助学生形成探索、研究、创新和创造的能力。在这个过程中，高校教师必须开展学术研究，否则无法胜任人才培养的重任。中小学老师面对的是不同的教学对象，承担不同的教学任务。举个最简单例子，1+1＝2，这是最基础的算术题，小学老师在课堂上所做的是如何以有效的方式让学生学会计算，掌握这些最基础的知识，而不是去研究为什么1+1＝2。教师的工作是如何让学生有效地掌握这些知识，根据学生心理特征和认知特点组织教学，帮助他们成长成熟。中小学教师以学生的发展为中心，本职工作是教学，花费太多时间精力去开展研究、发表论文也不太现实。当然，中小学教师有好的经验要总结、交流，我也不反对他们写文章、搞教改，但必须以教学为主导，即开展教学改革、撰写论文的目的是为了教学，基于教学且服务教学。

记者：大家常说，英语教育领域的研究和实践之间存在很大的差距。您认为国内也是如此吗？如果是，我们该如何进行研究以更好地指导实践？

王守仁：中国英语教育研究相对薄弱，用以指导实践的研究成果不多。中国有数以亿万计的学生在学习英语，是最大的英语教育实践场地，但是基于实践的原创性理论还不多。可喜的是，近年来这种情况有了改观，许多优秀的学者站在中国土地上，解决我国外语教学中出现的真问题、急问题，解决方案能融合中外理论精华，有创新之处，并且能够与国际学界对话，这方面的突出代表是广外的王初明教授和北外的文秋芳教授。王初明教授从"以写促学"到"以续促学"，再到"续"论，深入探讨语言学习的本质机制，不断提炼升华理论。"续"活动是将输入与输出有机融合的手段，可以提高外语学习效率。有关"续"的研究成果已经陆续在国际杂志上发表，引起国外学者高度关注。文秋芳教授的"产出导向法"包括教学理念、教学假设、教学流程三个部分：教学理念包括"学习中心说""学用一体说""关键能力说"；教学假设涵盖"输出驱动""输入促成""选择性学习""以评为学"；教学流程由驱动、促成和评价若干循环构成。"产出导向法"致力于解决我国外语教学中"学用分离"的弊端，通过与国际学者多次对话，已产生了较好的影响。我和文秋芳教授合作基于"产出导向法"开发编写的《新一代大学英语》（*iEnglish*）系列教材已在全国多所高校使用,受到师生好评,取得了良好成效。中国英语教育领域有一批优秀学者正在积极探索,努力构建具有中国特色和国际可理解的原创英语教学理论。我相信在不久的将来,研究和实践之间的差距(the gap between research and practice)会越来越小。

国际英语教育中国大会
Global English Education China Assembly

杨鲁新

杨鲁新,教授,博士生导师,国务院特殊津贴专家,北京外国语大学英语学院副院长,中国外语教材研究中心副主任,中国英汉语比较研究会写作教学与研究专业委员会副会长,中国英汉语比较研究会外语教师教育与发展专业委员会常务理事,中国高等教育学会外语教学研究分会秘书长,教育部职业院校外语类专业教学指导委员会委员。主要研究方向包括语言课程与教学、第二语言写作教学、外语教师教育及学术读写能力发展。目前担任《基础外语教育》期刊主编、*Language Teaching Research* 编委、多家知名国际期刊的审稿专家。

以专业发展提升英语教师素质

北京外国语大学杨鲁新教授专访

记者：为什么英语教师的专业发展很重要？

杨鲁新：人才培养是国之大计，而人才培养的质量在很大程度上受到教师水平的影响。特别是在基础教育阶段，学生年龄偏小，各方面都处于迅速成长的时期，也是最容易受到教师影响的时期。也就是说，教师的素质将直接影响学生的品性养成和综合素质发展。毋庸置疑，教师质量决定一个国家的教育水平。因此，教师需要不断地进行专业发展，从而能更好地服务学生。目前，由于我国各地区的教育基础不同，教师素质也出现了参差不齐的现象。

从英语学科来讲，据我所知，东部、西部、西北及西南之间的差异较大。每一个地区内都有重点学校和普通学校，其师资水平是存在差异的。虽然国家出台了一些好的政策，但是因为教师素质（如缺乏较强的英语基本功、不熟悉外语教育教学理论）达不到要求，许多政策很难真正落实，无法实现英语课程标准要求学生达到的综合能力和素质培养目标。因此，要大力提升我国人才的素质，一定要从教师教育方面入手。我认为，基础教育质量的提高需要高校的积极参与。我国高校英语学科专业（特别是师范院校的英语学科专业）相关负责人、教师等要经常下校调研，真正了解目前学校在英语教学、英语教师发展中存在的实际问题，从而更加有针对性地制定出职前和在职英语教师的培养方案，设计相应的课程，采用符合成人学习特点的教学方法或教学活动，从而从根本上提升英语教师素质。

记者：教师的专业发展体现在哪些方面？在不同方面分别有哪些途径可以提高自己？

杨鲁新：教师发展主要体现在专业能力、教学能力和反思能力。专业能力指教师的英文水平、教师自身的听说读写译能力。不论是在教中学还是小学，教师除了阅读教材以外，还应不断地大量阅读英文书籍，这样才能持续提高自己的专业能力；其次是教学能力。教学能力的提升不是简单地能够在讲台上教课，而是需要去研读一些语言教与学方面的理论书籍，观摩同事的教学，或者自己上研究课，在这个过程中不断实践适合学生水平的教学方法，理解语言学习的本质。当然，最重要的一点是反思能力。虽然每天都很忙，教师还是每天要抽出点时间反思自己的教学：今天的课上出现了什么问题？什么地方做得很好？什么地方做得不足？只有及时反思，教师才能够不断进步。

记者：您认为现在英语教师在专业化方面普遍的缺点是什么？

杨鲁新：我觉得目前英语老师最缺乏的是对语言学习本质的认识。正因为不太了解语言学习的本质，很多教师的教学活动是违背语言学习规律的，这表明教师没有真正理解学生、理解学习。语言学习与学生的认知年龄是紧密相关的。只有采取符合学生认知年龄、符合语言学习规律的方法，才能真正促进学生语言学习的发生。在我们的教师培训中，可能给教师传授了很多方法、很多活动，但是在促使教师对每个方法、每个活动背后原理真正理解方面则做得不到位或低效。只有真正理解这些原理时，教师才能在教学中做到举一反三。很多时候，通过观摩课，教师学到了一个方法（如组织小组活动），也在自己的课上实践了，效果可能很好，也可能没有达到预期，但是教师不清楚接下来需要做哪些事情，这就说明教师并没有理解这个方法所遵循的学习规律。因此，我认为教师培训需要在语言学习本质、学生学习规律、学生学习特点等方面下功夫。当然，教学方法最好是案例式教学，而不是空洞的理论说教。

记者：英语考试社会化趋势对日常教学有何影响？教师应学习哪些新东西来应对这些变化？

杨鲁新：我认为最核心的一点是教师要了解社会化考试的类型与内容，做到知己知彼。现在社会化考试越来越多地考查学生的综合语言应用能力，如果再像以前那样教学生刷题，肯定不会取得好成绩。这又回到我刚才谈到的问题，最核心的还是要理解语言学习的规律。

现在的社会化考试迫使教师要遵循语言学习规律来开展教学,只有这样,才能让学生应对不同类型的考试。在语言教学中,教师不能仅仅教学生背单词,而是要让学生掌握词汇、语法、篇章结构,更重要的是运用这些知识。教师需要通过大量的阅读、写作和听说活动综合地培养学生的语言运用能力。如果教师的教法得当,引导得当,那么无论怎么考,学生都能应对。所以,教师也不要害怕考试,最重要的还是要研究学法、教法、学习的本质,这才是最核心的任务。

教师可能还需要多读一些理论书籍,否则就会人云亦云。这也是为什么很多教师看别人做什么,自己就做什么,因为他们没有理论功底,没有能够进行自我分析和正确判断的能力,也就很容易面对各种考试要求时感到紧张。如果遵循了学习规律,可能短时间内学生成绩未必能明显提高,但是只要坚持,学生的学习效果一定会很好。比如,教师让学生大量阅读、写作,而不是做题,经过一个学期的训练,学生的语言综合运用能力就会大幅度提升,怎么考都没有问题。因此,教师要抓住语言学习的核心,不能只看眼前的或者短时的效果,一定要遵从语言学习规律。

记者:在教师教育领域,一个由来已久的话题就是理论和实践的联结和转化问题。一线教师难以将理论转化为实践,教学模式化的问题也由此而生,您认为这背后的根本原因是什么? 教师该如何走出这一困境?

*杨鲁新:*理论与实践关系的背后对应的是两大主体阵营,一方是以高校教师为代表的研究者、教师教育者,一方是以中小学教师为代表的实践者。教师教育在预备未来教师和组织教师在职发展中都期待教师能加强理论与实践的互动和转化,成为联结理论与实践的积极建构者。但是,职前教师和在职教师都对理论有着天然的排斥。职前教师往往觉得所学理论知识与实习学校所实施的教学方法相悖。因此,许多职前教师往往面临不能顺利胜任教学工作的问题。其中,一些新手教师发现顺应学校现行做法是其最佳的生存之道。而在职教师因为工作量大,缺少时间和资源,少有阅读文献的习惯,而难以将理论成果迁移到教学实践中。

我们需要认识到,我国中小学外语教师大多数毕业于师范院校,少部分教师毕业于综合大学和外语类大学。为什么毕业于师范院校的教师仍存在理论与实践转化困难的问题呢？这与长期以来师范院校的外语专业缺乏明确的办学方向有关。许多师范院校的外语专业主要采用"外语专业缩略版"加"二学一法"（教育学、心理学和教学法）的模式，且有些师范院校还存在"去师范化"倾向，强调综合性和实践性，对培养学生学习"如何教外语"方面关注不够，如把原来的"英语教育"专业改为"英语""英语语言文学"等专业，去掉原来必修的教育学、教育心理学、外语教学法等课程。结果是，这些职前教师在高校学习期间就没有得到系统的有关语言教育的训练，缺乏对语言学习规律、语言学习理论的学习与深入理解。

　　教师在理论与实践的互动转化中还受其实践性身份定位的限制。教师接受和运用理论与其感受的理论有用性和相关性有关。我发现，教师更愿意借鉴一些与教学直接相关、便于操作的理念和方法。教师也往往将自己与专家、学者等区分开。教师对自身作为实践者的身份定位限制其对成为研究者、理论工作者的认识和追求，也直接影响其对理论与实践的理解及转化运用。这种实践性身份定位方式在外语教师群体尤为凸显。由于对外语教育的复杂本质认识不清，导致对外语教学的工具化和技能化理解倾向，致使外语教师在教学与科研之间产生冲突，对自己的专业前景和学科认同产生困惑。

　　破解理论与实践联结和转化问题需要教师重新认识自己的角色，即教师不是被动的知识接收者和理论应用者，而是能够自主反思、探究和积极建构知识的实践者和学习者，并在所处环境中有目的地运用理论甚至产出理论。各种教师培训或教研活动都应鼓励教师进行反思，提炼自己的教学实践智慧，积极学习有关语言学习、教育教学等理论，助力教师成长为转化型知识分子。

邹 斌

邹斌，获英国布里斯托大学英语教育博士学位，目前担任西交利物浦大学应用语言学系英语教育项目主任、博士生导师，中国语言智能教学专业委员会常务理事，中国外语教育技术研究会理事，中国科学技术史学会语言、文学与科学研究专业委员会理事，美国和英国两个国际学术期刊的创刊主编和联合主编。主要研究方向为英语教育、学术英语、外语教育技术及人工智能。出版专编著8部，在SSCI、CSSCI国内外期刊发表50多篇论文。

英语教学在人工智能时代的机遇与挑战

西安交通利物浦大学邹斌教授专访

记者：未来几年 AI 技术在中国英语教育改革领域将有哪些作为？AI 技术能替代教师吗？

邹斌：我认为 AI 将在我们国内英语教育中起到非常大的作用。随着技术的不断发展，它给我们英语教师提供了很多前所未有的帮助。比如，以往在教学过程当中，教师无法给学生很多及时的反馈，特别是在大班教学的情况下。而人工智能现在已经可以和个性化教学结合起来，可以给学生提供个性化的辅导。在我们的英语教学中，大部分是大班教学，教师在课堂上的时间非常有限，课下更没有时间对学生进行个性化辅导。而人工智能因其技术的先进性，可以通过大数据把学生的个性化特征、学习特点等形成一个完整的链条，对学生提供个性化的学习辅导。而我们的英语教师时间有限，地点有限，是无法做到这一点的。因此，我觉得人工智能可以在写作、口语测评等方面提供非常大的帮助。

人工智能可以提供个性化辅导，但是它不能代替教师，教师在课堂上的教学是人工智能技术无法代替的。还有师生之间的情感交流，人工智能也是达不到的。

记者：人工智能进入英语教育学科领域后，技术支持资源与教学环境的改变促使英语教学发生了一系列的转变。除了英语教与学的方式发生改变之外，您认为人工智能技术的应用对英语教育理念会产生什么影响？

邹斌：人工智能技术为学习者提供了更多个人辅导和练习的机会，通过大数据和输入机器的各种反馈内容，人工智能可以为不同的学习者提供个性化指导和个性化的学习资源,进行自主学习,并为学生的写作和口语练习进行打分和评论;同时还能提供模仿人类的对话练习,让学习者与虚拟人,如其他学生或教师,进行会话练习。因此,人工智能时代的课外学习和指导,不再是将人类教师作为唯一选择,相应的人工智能英语学习产品可以替代一些课后教师辅导的角色,也可以为教师的课堂教学提供一些辅助。

然而,人工智能技术始终是模仿人类教师的角色,远没有达到代替教师的水平。人工智能技术仍取代不了教师在课堂上的主要角色,但可以在课下承担一些教师的工作,减轻教师课下辅导和反馈的负担,也同时给学生更多练习和自我纠正的机会。

记者:人工智能在基础英语教育和高等英语教育阶段的应用有哪些不同之处?

邹斌:人工智能在基础教育阶段发展得比较快,提供的学习资源和学习反馈也比较丰富,对英语口语及写作的评分也比较准确。人工智能口语评测技术在一些地区的中考和高考英语口语考试中取代了教师的人工打分。然而人工智能在高等教育阶段的发展上还不尽如人意,因为高等英语教育代表了高水平的英语,具有开放性、多样性和复杂性,人工智能技术还无法实现像为基础英语教育那样提供准确评分和反馈,在技术和数据上仍需要突破,这也是难点。

记者:在"人工智能+"时代,英语专业教师面临着哪些机遇和挑战?

邹斌:英语教师在"人工智能+"时代主要面临两大挑战。第一,英语教师应该随着技术的发展不断学习新技术、新知识,运用人工智能技术辅助英语教学。然而,英语教师很难通过自己的学习掌握新技术和熟练运用新技术,这需要教育部门、学校和相关协会或机构提供不断的培训,才能实现让教师熟练运用人工智能技术于课堂辅助教学和教会学生课下自主学习。第二,在现有的人工智能英语学习产品中,教师很难找到相关的产品用于自己的课堂教学。无论人工智能技术发展得多么好,没有适合课堂教学的产品,教师也很难运用人工智能技术于英语课堂教学中,也无法安排学生在课下使用某款适合课堂教学内容的人工智能产品进行自主学习。而且,即使教师熟悉某个产品,也无法推荐给学生使用并辅助自己的教学,因为涉及缴费学习,这需要当地教育部门和学校集体采购。

记者:为应对人工智能技术带来的挑战,您认为英语专业教师应该如何紧跟时代步伐,调整自身角色来适应"人工智能+"时代的教育环境?

邹斌：一是教师要加强自我的终身学习，经常关注和参与各类培训，学习如何将人工智能技术运用于英语教学中，不要仅仅等待或拒绝接受新技术。因为未来的英语教学中，熟练运用技术的教师也许会慢慢取代不会运用技术的教师；同时，教师也可以学习和研究如何让人工智能技术为自己的教学服务，如可以和技术人员交流，把自己的想法告知技术人员，让他们协助开发相关产品应用于课堂教学和辅助学生课下自主学习；同时也需要了解一些市场上已经开发出的人工智能英语学习产品是否适合自己的教学，从而了解人工智能技术以及相关产品的优势和不足。

记者：人工智能固然在英语教育领域发挥很大的正面作用，但当前的技术水平使其在该领域的作用仍有其局限性。您认为当前人工智能技术在英语教育领域作用的局限性具体体现在什么地方？

邹斌：一是技术层面。虽然语音识别和语音评测已经达到一定的准确度，然而在识别英语的复杂性、不同的语音、不同的语言环境方面还远没有达到100%精准的水平，而且在周边有其他噪音的情况下，语音识别准确度也下降不少。因此，人工智能技术在多样的开放题目、复杂的语法和词汇，以及更复杂的语义、语用、内容及逻辑等方面，还很难给出像人类教师一样的评分和反馈。二是高水平英语大数据的收集及相应的机器学习也没有达到应用层面的需求，仍需要大数据和机器学习的支持。

记者：当前人工智能教育的众多产品和应用过于关注人工智能技术而忽略了教育内容、教育方法和教育模式的与时俱进，并没有在学习者的能力培养和提升方面产生显著效果。有研究表明，教育科技对学习效果的影响相当有限，并不比非技术的学习干预的效果更好。对此您有什么看法？

邹斌：因为人工智能公司虽然擅长技术，但对教育教学和语言特征缺乏详尽了解，并较少配合一线有经验的教师针对各地不同的课堂内容进行开发，只是简单应对一下课堂内容，因此无法遵循良好的教育方法和教育模式。同时现有技术也无法完全实现教学要求的效果；而且一些理念也需纠正，就是教育科技不是以取代教师为目的的，而是辅助教学的工具，提供相应的帮助，对学生也是提供额外辅导，不能取代课堂学习，因此不能期待太高。其次，由于一线教师对人工智能技术也缺乏了解，也不知如何更好地运用技术为自己的教学服务，即使有较好的技术和产品，也不一定能充分利用技术的优势,因此会出现懂技术的可能不太懂教学,懂教学的不太懂技术,两者缺乏桥梁和合作,双方都需要积累和合作。

记者:您认为人工智能技术在英语教育领域还有哪些应用前景?

邹斌:人工智能技术将来会给高水平和复杂的英语口语提供更准确的评分和更详尽的反馈,在将来也会理解复杂的语义和语用环境,也能提供更复杂的交互场景让学生进行自主对话练习并给予反馈;同时也可以根据学生的水平自动提供相应的听说读写练习,并提供及时反馈,不需要教师和学生自己去找相应的学习内容。智能教育的未来是既提供大规模学习,也提供个性化学习,运用大数据和机器学习,提供给学习者有针对性的学习内容和知识归纳及总结,并像人类教师一样提供详尽指导和反馈,以达到举一反三的目的,把辅助教学做得更加完善和有效。但它仍然是辅助教学,不能完全取代教师的课堂教学和与人类的交流。

第二部分

外籍专家访谈录

Hugo Baetens Beardsmore

Hugo Baetens Beardsmore is emeritus professor of English and Bilingualism at the Vrije Universiteit Brussel, Belgium, and of Sociology of Language at the Université Libre de Bruxelles, Belgium. He has worked as a consultant on issues connected with bilingualism, bilingual education and language planning for the European Commission, the Council of Europe, Singapore, Belgian and Brunei ministries of education, as well as the Basque(Spain), Catalan(Spain), State of California and Canadian government authorities, the Welsh Government (United Kingdom), the island of La Réunion and the Russian Federation. For the Council of Europe he has worked as an expert on the Language Education Policy Profiles for the Irish Republic and the Val d'Aoste Region of Italy.

He has published 6 sole-authored books, 2 co-authored books; edited 5 books, and published 143 articles, 10 reports for government agencies, and 12 book reviews. Most of his publications cover linguistic, educational, sociolinguistic and sociological questions connected with bilingualism. His books include: *Bilingualism, Basic Principles*, Clevedon, Multilingual Matters, 1986; *European Models of Bilingual Education*, Clevedon, Multilingual Matters, 1993; *Bilingual Education in the 21st Century: A Global Perspecitve* (with Ofelia Garcia), Chichester, Wiley-Blackwell, 2009.

Bilingualism, Education and English

An Interview with Hugo Baetens Beardsmore

Reporter: Do you remember how you became bilingual?

Hugo Baetens Beardsmore: I was born in the town hall of a small village in Belgium, where the mayor delivered me and immediately entered my name in the registry as the first birth of the year, stating that this augured well for my future. I was not brought up as a "simultaneous bilingual" with two languages from birth, as my only home language was a Flemish dialect of Dutch. My father died before I was 2 years old and my mother married an Englishman a few years later, so when we moved to England I began to learn English. I had started school in Dutch in Belgium and moved straight into an English school on arrival. Hence I became an "early consecutive bilingual" though I have no recollections of learning English. There was a time when I could not speak the language and a time when I could, though I remained strongly influenced by my family's Flemish dialect and my mother's unidentifiable accent in English, which everyone found charming.

Reporter: Is your own family bilingual?

Hugo Baetens Beardsmore: Partially, yes. I was often perturbed when people asked what my "mother tongue" was since the term is ambiguous, as it may imply "language first learnt, language best known, most comfortable language, language of self-identity, etc., etc." (Byram, M. & Hu, A., 2013, p. 474–476). It may even

74

have sexist overtones and in provocation I would sometimes answer, "my father tongues are Dutch and English," depending on my two fathers, and I personally prefer to say that my preferred language depends on who I am interacting with, when, and where. One of my brothers spoke Dutch, English, French and German, though most other closer family members are more or less monolingual, though Belgians in general are pretty open to other languages, even if they may not master them well. For example, my cousins, who did not have any English lessons, communicate in broken English with English cousins, in French when tourists stop to ask the way and even in German if necessary.

Reporter: To what extent did "being bilingual" determine your choice of research area?

Hugo Baetens Beardsmore: I took to language learning with gusto at school and university, studying French, German and Italian, and picking up a feeling for Welsh as an undergraduate. My chequered personal linguistic development culminated in a doctorate based on bilingual influences (published as *Le français régional de Bruxelles*, 1971), which analysed the impact of Flemish dialect on Brussels French and led to my subsequent career.

Because of language policy implications, the publication of my Ph. D. thesis provoked much interest in the press in Belgium and France, with several half-page articles outlining the major findings, interviews on news, radio broadcasts and articles by members of parliament. The media were particularly interested in the historical evolution of the two languages in Brussels, developments in census statistics which changed the city from a Dutch language majority to a French-speaking majority, together with socio-linguistic explanations of what made Brussels French distinct from French elsewhere.

The specific characteristics of my research on language usage in the Belgian capital required field-work with representatives from all walks of life and led to many interesting and at times amusing recorded interviews. I had materials from different social categories, including prisoners in jail, patients in geriatric wards, beer-drinkers in popular cafés who mistook me for a health worker, a snooping private detective, a reporter, or a social security inspector, since some respondents could not imagine a person over 22 still "in school", as they put it. This type of field-work was backed up by intensive library research since the features that turned up had to be compared to standard Dutch as used in the Netherlands and standard French as used in Paris so as to discover how the deviations could be explained.

Many years later I was involved in directing a more complex investigation on language usage in Brussels, as the capital of Europe, to discover trends in the use of French or Dutch as the national languages among native Belgians and international migrants, including blue- and white-collar employees, civil servants and diplomats at the European Commission, the NATO Headquarters and the plethora of embassies. As this type of investigation was politically extremely sensitive, we had to be excessively careful to avoid any criticism on the methodology chosen, the training of interviewers, the representativity of the sample (3,000 subjects) and the presentation of results. Findings revealed the rate of changes in language usage across generations, the increase in bilingual skills, the use of either French or Dutch in official circumstances, the tendency to switch languages or not, and which languages those of foreign origin used according to their skills in French or Dutch. Results also led to the concept of a "default" language in a bilingual city, i. e. the language people fall back on in non-threatening circumstances, which may not be the case when linguistic identity or linguistic legislation is important.

Analysing my mother's use of English, the nature of my personal linguistic development, the questions raised as a result of my immigrant status in Britain, the problems of identification because of a "bilingual" surname, the research on Brussels and its bilingual status inspired me to offer a course on bilingualism to 4th year students of languages or education at the Flemish University of Brussels. The Faculty allowed me to introduce the course on the condition that it went under the title "Advanced course on the study of bilingual problems". This condition perturbed me, since I always felt that monolingualism was the problem, but I accepted, leading to the first course on bilingualism for undergraduates in Europe (1980), if not in the world. When interested students enquired as to which language I would use in the course I would sometimes reply, "Bilingual, of course!", given that participants came from different faculties and were sometimes of mixed or foreign origin. I also allowed them to choose the language of their oral examination if it was one I could handle. I have taught through the medium of English (English Linguistics), French (Sociology of Language) and Dutch (Explanation of Historical Texts) in different courses on the same day, and still regularly use all three at different times of the day. Students in Communication Sciences asked me to expand my course on "Terminology of the Anglo-Saxon Media" into a trilingual performance, claiming that they did not know the equivalent terminology in Dutch or French and the three languages would be useful in their future careers. I was not happy with this request, but students consistently voted it as a model example, primarily I believe because they had a boost of self-confidence in their receptive language skills.

Reporter: What led you to write your book *Bilingualism: Basic Principles*?

Hugo Baetens Beardsmore: My personal history, doctoral research, subsequent career as a specialist in French who taught English at university level, inspired the book *Bilingualism: Basic Principles* (1982, 1986), which, as the first publication by Multilingual Matters, sold well internationally, serving as a foundation source for a discipline that has considerably developed over time. My major goal was to show that bilingualism is NOT intrinsically a problem but an enrichment, that bilinguals statistically outnumber monolinguals on a world level and that misconceptions and research bias required a more scientific approach to its development. I also wanted to underline the interdisciplinary nature of work on bilingualism by covering not only purely linguistic aspects, but also sociological and psychological questions, educational, testing and policy issues and even the literary exploitation of bilingual situations. All these approaches have figured in my later work, the only regret being that I did not master statistics, given that today quantitative approaches tend to dominate, though I still maintain that these should be supported by qualitative approaches, given that we are dealing with human beings in varied situations with complex configurations.

Reporter: What positions did you want to defend in your book (and in later writings)?

Hugo Baetens Beardsmore: Initially the book aimed to clarify specifically what bilingualism is, under what different forms it existed and how speakers who knew more than one language used them, how they were perceived and what the consequences of being bilingual might be. For example, in one experiment I produced recordings of a monolingual native-speaker and a bilingual speaker's use of English for judgement by language students in Belgium, Britain and Germany. All respondents were asked for their personal definition of bilingualism, which most gave as, "the perfect knowledge of two languages," claiming themselves as non-bilingual. The majority of responses rejected the bilingual's English as not reflecting bilingual competence, even though most judged it acceptable and comprehensible. Since I have never come across a "perfect bilingual," or a "perfect monolingual," for that matter, the implicit value judgement for users of two languages reveals unconscious bias and impossible criteria.

In 1976 I was requested by the European Commission to investigate the educational problems confronted by parents whose careers led them frequently to change countries where schooling was not available in the initial home language of their children. The aim was to encourage employment mobility and internationalisation within Europe, so as to promote economic development. After visiting several pioneering schools in different countries confronted with the issue of educating children through two or three languages (cf. *European Models of Bilingual Education*, 1993), observations revealed that whether two or three languages were involved the linguistic issues were similar, though the contextual and pedagogic issues were more diverse, and more intricate. Some schools encouraged exclusively using one or the other language in different parts of the programme, whereas others either allowed some sort of switching, or even encouraged it as a help towards content learning.

Both my doctoral thesis and this first work with policy makers taught me a lot about the politics of language issues, the more so as I come from a country notorious for its language conflicts (cf. Witte, E. & Baetens Beardsmore, H., *The Interdisciplinary Study of Urban Bilingualism in Brussels*, 1987). Consequently I worked as a consultant to different governments and was requested to address parliaments on language planning and educational issues in a variety of contexts in Europe, Asia, Africa and the Americas.

Reporter: Who is (still) afraid of bilingualism nowadays?

Hugo Baetens Beardsmore: One of my most frequently requested lectures goes under the title of *Who's Afraid of Bilingualism* (2003), which I have delivered in Spain, Switzerland, California, Singapore, Germany, and Belgium. Such frequent requests reveal that in spite of progress in the understanding of some of the issues involved there is still a long way to go. The types of worries that come to light break down into the four categories of Politico-Ideological Fears, Educational Fears, Parental Fears and Cultural Fears.

Certain authorities base their reticence towards bilingual development on nationalistic ideologies which may foster or impede separatism, others on misgivings about the effects of bilingualism due to entrenched monolingual (superiority) complexes, others on familiarity with problem cases of language in education due to inadequate provision, catastrophic implementation strategies and social deprivation.

One factor is that most people feel they are experts in language and education because they all speak at least one language and have all been to school, hence basing their opinions for or against bilingual education on haphazard, personal or anecdotal evidence using simplified interpretations of complex issues. I have often been confronted by articulate opponents of bilingual education who have learnt to manipulate a second language through traditional language lessons and who tend to take their personal success as an example. They might thereby be ignoring their intellectual, social or educational privileges, treating as "losers" those who are confronted with difficulties in validating their experience with more than one language. This is particularly the case in a school system that might not promote successful exploitation of bilingualism, thereby hampering the climb up the social ladder.

Parental fears often come to the fore when a bilingual programme is offered for the first time. I regularly give evening talks all over the country to parent associations requiring reassurance about a bilingual initiative they are not familiar with. The sessions sometimes go on till midnight and I distinguish between regular general questions and more specific, private queries which I handle discretely afterwards. Parents often worry about which language to start teaching reading in, how they can contribute to homework when they don't know the target language, whether too much of the timetable being devoted to L2 will retard knowledge of the home language, how to organise non-scholastic outside activities in which language, etc. , etc. Answers to the above type of question must be carefully considered since the particular environment, the specific combination of languages, the nature of the curriculum, all have an influence and imply that there is no "one size fits all" answer.

For example, both English and French have very complex writing systems that do not easily reflect pronunciation, unlike Dutch, Italian or Spanish. In the particular context of French-speaking Belgian, bilingual schools can decide to start teaching young children how to read either in their first language, or in their second language, or in both at the same time, depending on teacher availability. Some French-speaking parents who enroll their young children in a bilingual programme where Dutch is the target language tend to worry when told that reading will first be taught in the easier Dutch only, leaving reading in French aside. After the first year these children are taught to read in French and to the parents' horror they hear their French-speaking children reading their first French texts aloud with a strong Dutch accent! This is a temporary development and after two weeks the teachers train the children to relate the French written script to their knowledge of French and the Dutch writing to their other reading language. Test results taken a few years later, at the end of primary school, reveal that the children involved in programmes that taught reading in the L2 first have native-speaker reading skills in their French home language, and advanced reading skills in Dutch. These positive results are better than in schools that select the alternative programmes.

Reporter: In your definition of bilingualism, you mention two (or more)

languages (or dialects). Does that mean that you consider bilingualism and multilingualism to be the same? Aren't there both quantitative and qualitative differences?

Hugo Baetens Beardsmore: In the specialist literature some authors refer to bilingualism as an umbrella term including the notions of bi-dialectism and multilingualism whereas others refer to multilingualism as including the sub-divisions of bilingualism and bi-dialectism. Distinctions between the different combinations are legitimate, depending on the aims of an analysis, since the whole area of investigation is marked by complexity, to use a currently fashionable term in research on language questions. One of the pioneers in the field, William Mackey (1976), claimed that over 3,000 variables could possibly intervene in a class implementing a bilingual education programme, making any analysis partial. Applied mathematicians are confronted with a similar problem when investigating phenomena such as "mass in a flow" (e. g., how particles in a liquid may affect viscosity, whether in water supplies or a weapon's firing efficiency). The issue of how precisely to define the phenomena of using more than one language depends on the major thrust of any investigation, given that there are certain points of similarity or difference between bilingualism and multilingualism, depending on the objectives of the study.

To take some examples from the educational sector. I have been involved in the promotion of Content and Language Integrated Learning, or CLIL, as a European term which covers various types of bi- or multilingual education programmes (cf. Marsh et al., 2002). In its promotion of greater mobility coupled with European integration, the European Commission has proposed encouraging all citizens to acquire what they designate as "Mother tongue plus 2 other languages" or M+2. The choice of CLIL to represent this format is a political decision resulting from an analysis of practice in the 27 member states; in some countries the words "bilingual education" are taboo; in others the Canadian designation of "immersion" is not accepted; in some the bilingual programme may cover teaching non-language subjects through the medium of two languages, while in others three languages may be involved, depending on the population make-up, language legislation or the level of instruction, which may differ considerably in primary, secondary or tertiary education. Luxembourg has no specific term to designate its official language programme which uses three languages at all levels of education for the entire population, merely referring to "education" in the way monolingual schools do elsewhere. The two universities of Brussels, one based on French, the other on Dutch as primary language of instruction, both oblige students following programmes in Business and Management Studies to follow some courses in which three different languages are distributed across distinct content-matter subjects, the two Belgian national languages and English.

Hence three sets of factors come into play in discussions on how to categorise programmes promoting more than one language; situational factors, which determine the context for language choices, operational factors, which determine the possible strategies required to use two or more languages in a curriculum, and outcome factors, which fix the targets and measurement tools used in a given programme's finality (Baetens Beardsmore, 2009).

My consultancy work with different ministries of education reveals how official authorities may or may not take two or three distinct languages into account in their education programmes. For example, the government of Brunei uses Malay, English and Arabic in its official school programmes; Malay as the cement of national cohesion, English for science and economic development and Arabic for religious reasons. However, some children do not have Malay as their home language but a distinct Borneo language, implying that they are confronted with four languages in their childhood. Bruneian children are also taught the use of Arabic script (*Jawi*) for Arabic and Malay and the Latin alphabet for both English and Malay, thereby adding a further parameter in the design of the school programmes. Privately run Chinese schools in Brunei use Chinese, English and Malay.

The special French regional government of La Réunion off the coast of Africa imposes a monolingual all-French programme of education, ignoring the fact that the majority of children have the distinct French Creole as their home language. Creole is minimally tolerated in a few pioneering programmes, serving as a stepping-stone towards a monolingual education system that ignores the linguistic reality of the island.

Kazakhstan is gradually building up a unique, predominantly bilingual programme for a population that is primarily made up of Kazakh or Russian home-language speakers. (The other regional languages present in some areas of the country will not be addressed here.) A simplified outline reveals that those with Kazakh as their home language receive content-matter lessons in Kazakh and English, and Russian in language lessons, those with Russian as a home language receive content-matter in Russian and English and Kazakh in language lessons. Two scripts complicate the process, since Kazakh and Russian use the Cyrillic script, though there are plans to use the Latin alphabet for Kazakh, alongside English (Nazarbayev Intellectual Schools, 2012).

A final example comes from the European School system, in use since 1958 for the children of European civil servants coming from different member states where all are expected to follow lessons in their major home language, a certain amount of content-matter through a second language and the compulsory choice of a third language from a range on offer. As the schools are divided into up to eight different linguistic-national sub-sections, all following the same curriculum and taking the same exams, irrespective of the base language of a particular group, this is a unique example of a multilingual programme following a predominantly bilingual curriculum, but where there is a great mixture of languages on each site. Anecdotally, parents are often amazed to hear their children speaking in a fourth or fifth language not part of their curriculum, but picked up from playground and friendship circles (cf. Flores, N. & Baetens Beardsmore, H. 2015).

Reporter: An interesting thing is that bilinguals will stay within one language when talking to monolinguals. However, when talking to other bilinguals, they will probably switch from one language to another. There are quite some misunderstandings regarding the phenomena of code-switching, code-mixing, and so-called "translanguaging." Some people believe that code-mixing or code-switching is a sign of linguistic deficit, a sign of laziness, or a sign of attempting

to show off on the part of a bilingual. What would you comment on this kind of belief?

Hugo Baetens Beardsmore: I was involved in an intensive three-year programme of research into code-switching involving about 250 scholars which led to 5 publications sponsored by the European Science Foundation, aiming to unravel the nature, prevalence and characteristics of different types of mixed language usage, according to context and competence (cf. Milroy, L. & Muysken, P. 1995). In no cases did code-switching (or translanguaging) reflect serious deficits, though they did show the effects of mixed code-usage on perceptions and attitudes. In only a few cases did the use of a combination of different language features reveal major inadequacies or handicaps, as when speakers were stigmatised, criticised or penalised for not sticking to a majority language in a specific environment.

Some bilingual speakers use elements from both languages in certain circumstances, usually when they know this will not impede communication with other similar bilinguals, whereas other bilinguals sharing the same combination may not do so, depending on the topic of discussion, the environment, the presence or absence of overhearers. Speakers who have not had sufficient opportunity to acquire a second language may inadvertently or deliberately have recourse to a "borrowed" first-language item or structure in a monolingual environment, at times leading to stigmatisation, but this is hardly different from inappropriate social etiquette conventions manifested by monolinguals in a non-familiar cultural setting. The current debate on translanguaging evolves round the emphasis given either to the *sociolinguistic* aspect of classroom language use or the norm-related *linguistic* issue of exit test measures for certification.

There is a growing concern among parents that bilingualism will delay language acquisition in children because they have to deal with two or more languages. Is there a valid reason to be worried?

The models examined and the in-depth research into code-switching revealed that properly designed bilingual upbringing, at home and at school, in no way impedes intellectual or behavioural development in children, on the contrary. Consequently parents confronted with the possibility of bringing a child up in two distinct languages from a very early age should normally not fear any deficiencies. (Cases of dyslexia or speech impairment are a separate issue and need adjustments, as in monolingual circumstances.) If the parents are not bilingual themselves they may note that their child can at times show different language usage patterns from those of a monolingual child, but such developmental differences normally represent nothing more than the bilingual having more choices, more options in language usage than a monolingual and hence needs to work out intuitively how to select the appropriate language and social interaction codes. Nevertheless, hastily imposed bilingual strategies, at home, at school and in society, coupled with prejudice and social deprivation, can lead to unfortunate failure and stress. Those involved in bilingual upbringing should be well-informed, well-trained, and well-supported, the more so if they are confronted with misapprehensions about multilingual skills. Two regional authorities in the United Kingdom (Wales and Scotland) provide information kits in pre-natal clinics on how to bring children up bilingually, considered just as important as other aspects of child-rearing for parents to-be.

Reporter: Are bilinguals also bicultural? Can someone be bilingual without being bicultural?

Hugo Baetens Beardsmore: Questions of language and culture can be at the origin of political discussions and *multilingual* countries with or without *plurilingual* citizens (to use the distinction used by the Council of Europe) have to produce language policies and language management strategies. Since a culture does not exist without a language, this raises questions on the relationship between bilingualism and biculturalism. It is possible for some individuals to be bilingual and bicultural, others are bilingual and monocultural, just as some people can be bicultural and monolingual. Several simple psychosocial tests can reveal these possibilities, for example, the word-association test, where subjects are asked to write down the first three words that come to mind on hearing a stimulus word. When Canadian monolinguals of either English or French heard the stimulus word "doctor (Eng.)/docteur (Fr.)", the majority of English-speakers responded with "nurse/patient" whereas the majority of French-speakers gave "sickness/health". These divergent responses might well reflect cultural differences. Bilinguals who were also bicultural gave similar responses to the English or French monolinguals respectively for the test taken in each language separately, whereas the bilinguals who were monocultural tended to give the same response in both languages. Other, more sophisticated tests, for example, the sentence-completion task, e. g. "When I quarrel with my wife... ", tend to evoke responses like, "the only solution is divorce" in young bilingual men in Arabic, with responses like, "I try to discuss the problem" by the more bicultural young men using their French. The monocultural people tend to give the same answer in both languages. (cf. Bentahila, A. , 1983).

Some studies have shown that if one knows two or more languages one may experience a delay in the onset of dementia (e. g. Alzheimer's disease). Can you share with us some major cognitive benefits of bilingualism/multilingualism?

In preparation for the European Year of Creativity (2009), I joined a team of researchers who were requested to provide an analysis of the relationship between multilingualism and creativity. This led us to analyse about 1, 500 studies revealing some perceptions on the issue and enabling us to arrive at tentative conclusions in favour of a positive relationship, but which require further more rigorously specific investigation.

The main positive features found include the following:

a. Bilingual children are better in tasks which require not the finding of the single correct answer to a question, but where they are asked to imagine a number of possible correct answers.

b. Bilingual children are better in tasks of divergent thinking. Some research into multilingualism and cognitive flexibility used tests where the subjects were asked to look at a picture which has more than one image embedded into it, and describe what they see. Bilingual children were more successful than monolinguals in seeing the other meaning in the images.

c. Studies on cognitive skills. Research in Italy and Switzerland has consistently shown intriguing differences in cognitive abilities; tests using L1 gave slightly better results on factual information, or "knowing what", whereas tests using L2 showed better results on *operational* information, or "knowing how" (Gajo, L. & Serra, C., 2002).

d. As for metalinguistic skills, there appears to be a greater understanding of how language is used to achieve specific goals in life involving understanding that words can have more than one meaning, identifying ambiguity, translating words and interpreting concepts, in other terms, using languages to learn, and learning to use languages, enabling the person to go beyond the words.

e. Studies on interpersonal relations reveal better understanding and responding to the communicative needs of others, contextual sensitivity and highly developed interactional competence in communication. Multilingualism is reported as helping to nurture interpersonal communication awareness and skills.

f. A tentative finding was that older bi- or multilinguals tended to manifest a two-year delay in the onset of dementia when compared with monolinguals. This requires further investigation.

Reporter: You were one of the first foreign scholars to be invited to lecture in China (Guangzhou) at the opening up of the country to foreigners in 1980. Can you share with us some interesting phenomena/incidents (relating to English language teaching and/or bilingualism) during your first visit to China? What shocked you most when you visited China for the first time? What shocked you when you visited China for a second time?

Hugo Baetens Beardsmore: My work for the European Commission gradually led to invitations to help develop language policy strategies, particularly in education, in different parts of the world, including the World Bank in Washington, the California State Department of Education, the Canadian Government, the Basque and Catalan Regional Governments in Spain, the Governments of Singapore and Brunei, and led thus to insights into multilingual issues in highly divergent contexts.

One of my most interesting missions came from the Hong Kong authorities in 1986 to help prepare the language education issues for 1997. I suggested a trilingual programme teaching through the medium of Cantonese, *Putonghua* and English by taking inspiration from the Luxembourg model in place since 1913, and where the whole school population is educated through three languages, leading the Prime Minister of Luxembourg to state that "Multilingualism is our mother tongue", given that Luxemburgish, a small and partially standardised language, is the only symbol to distinguish its citizens from its neighbours (*L'Avenir du Luxembourg*, 1989). Statistics regularly collected on the European level reveal interesting and contradictory findings on the relationship between language and the economy. Luxembourg has one of the highest standards of living per capita in the world and teachers are extremely well paid! 98% of the population claims to be competent in the use of three or more languages, the highest score in Europe (*Special Eurobarometer*, 2012). Luxembourg does less well in comparative measures of skills in science, mathematics and literacy for 15-year-olds than many other countries, though this could perhaps be partially attributed to a handicap through the very high number of immigrant children from different language backgrounds in the school system and the fact that the tests imposed may have to be taken in the second, third or fourth language of the pupils involved, where this is rarely the case elsewhere. However, the same statistics for autonomous regions in Italy (the Val d'Aoste with a bilingual education programme in Italian and French for all children), in Spain (the Basque Country using Basque and Spanish for all; the Catalan region using Catalan and Spanish for all) revealed better results on the three measures tested than those for the national states in which they were embedded. A comparison made in 2009 on the PISA (OECD international student assessment) tests for 15-year-olds on reading, mathematics, and science showed how the bilingual/trilingual systems often scored better than the monolingual schools in the countries these autonomous regions belonged to.

	Reading	Maths	Science
OECD mean	493	496	501
Basque Country (Spain)	494	488	482
Catalonia (Spain)	498	496	497
Spain	481	483	488
Val d'Aoste	514	502	521
Italy	486	483	489
Luxembourg	472	489	484

My attempts to allay reticence about the use of Cantonese, *Putonghua* and English in Hong Kong were not successful, yet the social and educational issues involved still exist.

Another exciting mission was in 1980, when I was the first foreign scholar to lecture in Guangzhou. I spent the mornings lecturing to hundreds of students in French and the afternoons in English and was amazed at the enthusiasm of the staff and students, who had not seen a foreigner for years. Equipment was very basic, books were scarce and the library pitifully empty, with the few dictionaries available chained up so as not to disappear. The thirst for knowledge and skills was inspiring, some of the students putting many questions on the nature of programmes abroad and I was struck by the fact that the students I spoke to were sometimes more fluent and had better accents than their teachers. On my return to Guangzhou 20 years later I was impressed by the progress and prosperity everywhere apparent. Language skills were just as high and as prevalent as during my first visit, but equipment and materials were as up-to-date as anywhere and there was a greater atmosphere of well-being. I was hence a witness to a success story in the making!

Reporter: At the request of Belgian Radio you broadcast a daily language spot for two years on how to improve English skills. Can you share with Chinese EFL learners some interesting bits of your broadcasting experience?

Hugo Baetens Beardsmore: During my missions to different language planning authorities, e. g. , in Kazakhstan or the Republic of Ireland, I frequently suggested using the media to inform the public on language learning skills. We in Belgium had considerable experience in encouraging people to improve their language usage, via the printed press, television and radio. Newspapers regularly printed tips on how to avoid dialect features in standard language, and there was a professor on television who became so popular with his friendly advice on Dutch that he ended up being elected to the senate.

I was invited to produce a daily language tip in English on Belgian radio and the broadcasting authorities knew exactly how to target their listeners. My two-minute tip was introduced by a lively signature tune and inserted just after 6: 30 p. m. between the news bulletin and the weather forecast, with the knowledge that audiences tended not to switch off or change channels until they had heard the weather bulletin. The same tip was broadcast daily for two years on the classical music channel towards 10: 58 p. m. since audience research had shown that that was when many teachers tuned in to the news before going to sleep.

With this knowledge I tended to keep my tips friendly and easy to digest, specifically covering language features not handled in standard courses, but which I thought were useful for easy communication. For example, I indicated some of the differences between British, American, Australian, Irish English. I often gave pronunciation hints, so as to avoid "spelling pronunciations". For example, I pointed out that "p" in words like "psychology, psychiatry" is not pronounced, that the "r" in "iron" is not pronounced, that the second "b" in "bomb, bombing" is not pronounced, as many learners make mistakes of this type. The topics also covered socio-cultural features of language usage, such as avoiding the use of clichés like, "And last, but not least...", frequently over-used by foreigners and which native-speakers often find irritating. I pointed out differences in the way men and women tend to use the language, particularly since many teachers of English were women and their language preferences made their men students occasionally sound strange. For example, women use adjectives like "exquisite, adorable, divine, sweet, pretty" more often than men, whereas men tend to use terms like "great, fantastic, very good" in similar contexts. Some of my broadcasts handled mistakes regularly made by Dutch or French-speakers of English, particularly "false friends" like the word "library" being mistakenly used to mean "bookshop". A similar programme for Chinese users of English could help ensuring that they mark final consonant sounds accurately, e. g. final "s" to distinguish singular from plural nouns, or the third person present of the verb, e. g. "she likes". This is one of the most frequently heard mistakes of Chinese users of English and is also the source of caricatures of Chinese users of the language in humorous sketches.

Gradually, listeners would write in to request a piece of advice on a particular feature of English and over time some wrote to the broadcasting station to request a printed version. This led to a modest publication, *Hints on English Usage* (*1975*), which sold well for several years. Given that this was an informal collection of observations and comments based on an oral delivery, the book was not intended as a serious academic text.

I subsequently took part in a combined radio and television series aimed to promote the learning of English, particularly for people who had little contact with the language in school. This was accompanied by a course-book and a series of audio cassettes with written and spoken exercises. As with my radio talks, the aim was to be amusing and useful, to capture a less intellectual audience by creating characters in every-day circumstances.

The unexpected success of these programmes leads me to encourage students learning English to take advantage of the massive technical revolution afforded by the internet, something that did not exist when I did most of my teaching. No matter how good a textbook may be, how proficient teachers are, how well equipped in technical support a school or institution may be, there is nothing like personal interaction, personal initiative to expand one's language skills, particularly the cultural and intonation features. I always recommend learners to take every opportunity to practise their languages as this is the best way to progress, even if it requires some tenacity, especially if your listener switches to your stronger language on the mistaken assumption of helping out.

Joy Egbert

Joy Egbert is Professor of English Language Learning and Education Technology at Washington State University in Pullman. She is also currently the editor of *TESOL Journal*. She has published and presented widely in the areas of teacher education, computer-assisted language learning, task engagement, and teaching methods.

New Technology and the Future of Language Teaching

An Interview with Joy Egbert

Reporter: What are your thoughts on the development of English education in China?

Joy Egbert: Actually, I haven't been in the largest cities in China before, and I'm impressed. It's my first time being alone in China, and I've had to ask a lot of questions and ask for directions. Everybody, even the cleaning women and people who are sweeping the street, knows a little bit of English. It's really impressive that anybody can help me. And I think about, if a Chinese person came to the United States, would anybody be able to help him? The answer is no, because we don't speak Chinese, and I think it's a real lack. And I'm happy to see that so many people do speak English here, just for my own even personal use.

Reporter: From what you've seen so far in China, what has impressed you about Chinese technology?

Joy Egbert: That is, everybody uses technology constantly. WeChat is probably the biggest platform in the world, right? And they use it for everything; video, it's Facebook, it's Twitter, it's all those things here. And my hope is that people will start thinking about using it for teaching, because it's a great tool to have people interacting in English, and you know, there are lots of different ways that they can use it. So, but that it's so prevalent and the technology for this conference is mind-blowing. It's beautiful. We don't have anything like it at my university, so it's amazing.

Reporter: Besides working as an English professor, you also recently completed a term as Editor of the *TESOL Journal*. So could you just explain to us what that is exactly?

Joy Egbert: TESOL has two journals. One of them is *TESOL Quarterly*, and that's known really around the world. It's one of the best journals to publish in for English education research or second-language research, and it's very highly regarded, SSCI. It focuses more on, I wouldn't say, pure research, but I think it's more of a high level of basic research with not as much application. And the *TESOL Journal* requires not only the same level of rigor, but in addition, some kind of application to teaching. So it's meant for researchers and teachers rather than just researchers.

Reporter: And what kinds of essays or papers does the journal accept?

Joy Egbert: There are generally six categories, but these change, so if readers go to the submission guidelines on the tesol. org website, they'll see what they are. Basically there are two kinds of feature articles: one is empirical with pedagogical implications, and the other is conceptual. So a lot of times, people look at a theory, or they look at a concept, and they apply it to teaching. And teachers need that kind of information. It's kind of like what I did today in my talk. There are other categories, for example, for graduate students. We ask for a two or three-minute video explaining about the studies that they're working on. There's also a category for current issues, and a lot of issues, of course in China, would fit perfectly in that category. So there're a variety of different kinds of articles to choose from.

Reporter: So how do you think people who work in the field of English teaching and research, how would they benefit from Chinese teachers' essays or papers or research?

Joy Egbert: I think it's that we all benefit by having a conversation about what works in our classrooms. Clearly, with all these people speaking English, something really good is going on in the country. And that they reach such a high level of English, I think, can inform people around the world. And the readers of *TESOL Journal* are around the world. They're global.

Reporter: Interesting and interactive classroom tasks are essential for keeping students fully engaged in lessons. How do you think English teachers in China can effectively use computer and Internet technology to design good classroom tasks?

Joy Egbert: It's about knowing students first and understanding what engages students, then designing the task according to what facilitates task engagement. According to the research literature, student interest, task authenticity/value, and social interaction are among the most important engagement facilitators. So, if I know that my students need to learn past tense, and that they're really interested in music from England, as a task I might try (or have them try) to find lyrics from British songs that are in past tense as a reading or example for them. They can listen to the pronunciation of the past tense by listening to the songs online, too. Then I can provide them with exercises and questions based on the past tense that integrate statements about the songs. In this way, I'm piquing their interest, making sure they understand that they are learning language (so it's an authentic task), and providing them with ideas that they can talk about. This all would be very difficult to accomplish without technology. That doesn't mean that tasks without technology aren't engaging, but there are so many more opportunities to offer students when technology is available.

Reporter: With foreign language teaching going into smaller cities and rural areas in China, how do you think technology can be used to help rural English education in such places where resources are relatively scarce?

Joy Egbert: There are some interesting papers and books about the use of technology for language learning in places with fewer technology options. Truly, all it takes is an internet or Wi-Fi connection and a creative teacher, and the sky's the limit! It's really amazing, for example, what can be done just with cell phones, which most people have these days. For example, dialogue journals can be conducted between the teacher and a student through voice or text and provide modelling of authentic pronunciation and grammar. Learners could do a write-around on a topic that they're interested in (while focusing on appropriate grammar) by each adding a sentence or two to a text message that is forwarded among learners. Learners can use their phones to listen to podcasts about academic topics, or the teacher can email them lecture notes, readings, and feedback.

In classrooms with no phones but access to an office suite (such as Microsoft Office or other free versions), learners can complete tasks like easily providing each other with comments on their written work, sharing graphics developed as an assessment of reading comprehension, and discussing the errors that the word processing program finds in a document.

Much has even been written about the "one computer classroom. " Not only can that one computer provide the teacher with all kinds of resources, it can serve as the focus of group language tasks (especially games), provide examples of native-like spoken English around topics that interest the learners, and broadcast graphics to initiate writing and discussion tasks.

If teachers think about how learners typically use the phone or other digital device, what they like to do on it, and what they might find authentic for language learning, any number of engaging tasks can be created. Likewise, because learners may be more familiar with the devices and the applications on them than teachers, having the learners suggest or help create tasks would insure that the tasks are interesting and authentic. My advice is for teachers to network with peers, search for useful technology-enhanced tasks that abound on the internet and in books and journals, and try tasks out for themselves. The thing to remember is that the lack of technology is no excuse for not engaging learners.

Reporter: Technology is still evolving. Do you think teachers will be replaced by technology someday in the future? What are your expectations for the future of digital education?

Joy Egbert: Generally, until artificial intelligence (AI) is cheap, ubiquitous, and creative, there's no chance that it can or should replace most teachers (I say most because some teachers are not as effective as some technology applications). To date,

AI does not meet these criteria—it can't jump into a conversation and correct learners, it can't understand the creative use of language in an essay, and it can't give creative feedback. Therefore, I don't expect to see technology replacing teachers anytime soon, and most of the field agrees with this claim.

Technology is evolving, but in schools much less so. Many language programs in schools in the US are using outdated hardware and ineffective software, and there are others in which the Internet is spotty. That said, the technology future is bright for teachers and students who can access it. New technologies are taking into consideration the facilitators of task engagement and what teachers need, and they are providing platforms that are more inclusive, more social, and more adaptable for all kinds of learning. These include applications that integrate different aspects of open-content software like document co-writing, group drawing, and social media/resource integration. In addition, recent assessment programs like Kahoot provide a variety of ways and modes in which teachers can assess, making the assessment more authentic and more interesting for students. Further, Padlet and other gallery software help students share and comment on each other's work. Even more recently, powerful digital social reading software like Hypothesis and Perusall allows collaborative reading and supports not only increased comprehension but shared understandings and interaction around text. Education technology is definitely moving in a more social direction, and I expect it to continue to do so. Also, because these apps are available on mobile devices, learning can take place through them without an actual physical "place", and there is no reason to think that this trend will stop. In other words, I think that the future of technology in education will be to facilitate anyone to be engaged in learning anywhere, even more so than currently!

Rod Ellis

Rod Ellis, PhD, is currently a research professor at the School of Education at Curtin University in Perth, Australia. He is also a visiting professor at Shanghai International Studies University and an Emeritus Distinguished Professor of the University of Auckland. He was recently elected as a fellow of the Royal Society of New Zealand and has written extensively on second language acquisition and task-based language teaching. His most recent book is *Reflections on Task-Based Language Teaching* (2018) published by Multilingual Matters.

Task-Based Language Teaching and Its Challenge in China

An Interview with Rod Ellis

Reporter: What do you think of the role of English language education in the communication between different countries and cultures?

Rod Ellis: We all live in a global world these days. This requires that we have a lingua franca—a language that we can communicate across global communities. And at the moment that language is English. But who knows, in another fifty years, it might be Chinese!

Reporter: How has the exchanges and mutual learning between different countries and civilizations changed over recent years? What are the influences of such changes on English education?

Rod Ellis: I think one thing that we need to recognize is that many parts of the world have always been multilingual. That is to say, people living in them have learned many languages. I think China perhaps is different from some other parts of the world, because by and large people learn just one language—Mandarin or a local dialect. But if you go to Africa, for example, even your ordinary person may speak three or four different languages. It seems to me that being bilingual is becoming more and more important. And as I said in the answer to the first question, at the moment English functions as the language of global communication and therefore, obviously, it's very important that people do learn English. This is very clearly recognized in China, where parents are very keen to ensure that their children start learning English from a very young age.

Reporter: Do you observe some other new opportunities in English language education?

Rod Ellis: The new opportunities are really coming from technical sources and the fact that people can not only learn English face-to-face but also through their mobiles or the Internet. In fact, I'm involved with a company in Beijing to try to develop an English language program for very young children, three years plus. The idea is that that program will be entirely online. Technology is going to have an enormous influence on the teacher and learning of foreign languages.

Reporter: As a guest professor at SISU, have you observed any new changes of Chinese students learning English?

Rod Ellis: My experience of China is that, where English is concerned, there appear to be two different groups of people. There are those Chinese people who can speak English not always perfectly but who are communicatively proficient. And then there are those people who can't communicate in English at all. If I walk into the restaurant, and I talk to some of the waitresses or waiters there, by and large, they can't speak English. On the other hand, if I meet educated people in Shanghai or Hangzhou or Beijing, then yes, not only can they speak English, but it seems to me that increasingly they can speak very good English. I have a lot of experience of working in Japan as well as working in China. And my impression is that English proficiency of those people who can speak English in China is increasing and is very high, in comparison to Japan. On the other hand, just about everybody in Japan can say a few words in English and I don't find that in China.

Reporter: With China having an increasingly important role in the world about English language teaching, do you see any Chinese wisdom or experience or theories generated here that can be applied globally or in other markets?

Rod Ellis: As I have just said, I meet Chinese people whose English is really very proficient. What interests me is how they've achieved that proficiency. I often talk to them about that. And what emerges is that all those with a high level of proficiency didn't just get it from studying in a classroom. They got it from what they did outside the classroom—watching videos, using the Internet to access English materials, joining English conversation groups, etc. I think this is becoming more and more common. I don't think it is just true to China. I think it's probably true throughout the world. Good language learners know that they cannot achieve high levels of proficiency by just relying on what goes on inside the classroom. It's what they are doing by themselves outside the classroom that matters. If students have motivation—and many Chinese students are very highly motivated to learn English—they will look to use the resources available to them outside the classroom to help them.

Reporter: Does such a phenomenon discourage other English educators because it kind of suggests that their work as classroom teachers is not so important?

Rod Ellis: Well, the classroom is important because it can provide learners with a start to build on. To my mind, the focus in the classroom should be the development of foundational communicative ability. But that's often not what goes on, certainly not traditionally in Chinese classrooms where the focus is less on developing a fundamental communicative ability and more on developing the ability to pass traditional language tests which prioritize accuracy and do not really tap into communicative ability. My approach is to ensure a fluency-first approach in the classroom rather than what we find at the moment, namely an accuracy-first and fluency-may-be-never approach.

Reporter: You just mentioned that you find Chinese English learners are highly motivated. Do you think they are more motivated than their counterparts in other countries?

Rod Ellis: Again, if I were to compare the level of motivation that I see in many students in China with similar students in Japan, I would have to conclude that overall it is higher in China. I think that high level of motivation originates in the students' parents. Because parents, particularly in middle-class families, prioritize the learning of

English, their children try to please them by trying hard. Many children, however, do become interested in learning English for themselves. They can see that it will give them a career path—perhaps as teachers but also in business. So, in China, we definitely do see a high level of motivation in learners. On the other hand, I also know that there are students who are not really very keen on learning English and only motivated to learn enough English to pass the tests they need to get into whatever university they want to or when at university to pass the tests needed to graduate. There are articles which indicate that the level of motivation of such students is actually quite low. They are likely to forget what they have learned soon after they have passed the tests. So clearly, the level of motivation in learners is going to be mixed. In general, though, I see students in China who are strongly motivated to learn English and consequently develop a very high level of communicative ability in English. And that, I think, is an excellent thing. It is not unique to China, though. I have witnessed very high levels of English proficiency in other countries, such as Iran.

Reporter: Aside from the sheer growing size of the foreign language learning market here in China, what other changes are you seeing?

Rod Ellis: One change is obviously the growth of private language schools in China. I've visited several of private language schools and found them very professionally run. So that is one obvious development that has taken place. The second development is emergence of companies interested in developing online English language programs for students. What we are seeing in China is the commercialization of English language teaching. China, of course, has the advantage of companies with large amounts of money to pour into the commercialization of language teaching. As this happens it is important to make sure that fundamentals are not lost sight of. And the most fundamental thing about language learning is not the learning materials that commercial language companies sell but what the individual learner does with the materials. Good materials by themselves do not ensure that learning is successful.

Reporter: Would the commercialization have an impact on how the educators and learners interact?

Rod Ellis: One hopes that the commercialization of English language teaching will lead to a general growth in language proficiency amongst the Chinese population. And perhaps that will happen. China is a huge country and very varied. Now when we look out of the window here we see a very beautiful modern city, Hangzhou. But we can go to other parts of China which are relatively undeveloped. We can go to schools where there are possibly no teachers with the proficiency needed to teach English. So if I was to say what I would really like to see happen, it is not the commercialization of English language teaching which will benefit the middle-classes, but an investment in the human resources needed to make it possible for children to learn English throughout this large country, not just in large commercial centers like Hangzhou, Shanghai, Beijing, etc. I guess in that respect, I'm a socialist.

Reporter: Foreign language teaching is moving into smaller cities and rural areas of the country where people speak strong dialects and some of them do not even speak standard Mandarin. Do you think there will be more challenges of English language teaching?

Rod Ellis: The crucial factor will be the availability of teachers with sufficient proficiency in English to teach. I don't know what policy exists regarding the training of teachers. Is there any requirement that teachers should first serve in rural areas or smaller towns once they have finished their government-funded training? If English is going to spread beyond the middle-class and beyond the larger urban centers of China, then there has to be a policy that will ensure that teachers are available in these rural, less urbanized centers. One possibility might be to provide a financial inducement for teachers to work in rural areas. I do not see the local dialect or the lack of Mandarin as an impediment to learning English if English is taught as a communicative tool.

Reporter: For those learners who are not exposed to foreign cultures from a very early age as the urbanized are, do you think it will be more difficult for them to learn English?

Rod Ellis: I don't think you need to be exposed to foreign cultures in order to learn a language. I mean, my teaching career started in Africa in the 1960s. I was posted in a very rural secondary school, very, very rural, 300 miles from the nearest tar road. And the children in that school had very little experience of other cultures other than the ones that they had grown up with at home. But many of them developed an extremely high level of proficiency in English. In fact, there was one particular boy at that school, whom I still think of as the most proficient second language learner that I've ever come across. So, I think it's a fallacy that one needs to have exposure to foreign language cultures in order to learn English. You can learn English in any setting, in any situation, if you want, if you have good teachers and well-designed materials to help you learn and know how to make effective use of them. I doubt whether there is a strong connection between exposure to foreign cultures and the learning of English. Not that the two cannot go together, but I do not think it is essential. What is essential is exposure to plentiful input.

Reporter: Is there a best age to learn a second language?

Rod Ellis: Well, of course, what we're seeing in China and in other countries throughout Asia is the introduction of the teaching of English in primary schools. I think that this does raise the question as to whether starting early is going to lead to substantial improvement in proficiency in the long term. What the research suggests is that starting young in a foreign language situation like China is not necessarily advantageous and may not lead to higher levels of proficiency later on. This is because, in a foreign language situation, the one advantage that children have, which is the ability to learn naturally, to learn implicitly, cannot be taken advantage of easily because they will need massive amounts of input to enable them to learn in that particular way and this may not be available. So in foreign language situations, starting young may not be so advantageous. On the other hand, parents are very keen to see their children start young, and I doubt that any government is going to want to displease parents by not giving them that particular opportunity. What I would suggest is that if you want to start introducing English into the primary schools, you need to conduct studies to evaluate to what extent it is successful. Projects that have investigated the introduction of foreign languages in other countries like Britain or Spain suggest that foreign language education in the primary school is nothing like as successful as people think it is.

Reporter: What is the key to success, then?

Rod Ellis: There are two keys to success, one of which I've already mentioned. The first is that learning a language at school in the classroom must be motivating so that students look forward to their English classes. And the second is what they do outside the classroom—getting access to English language learning materials outside the classroom and maximizing their exposure to English input. This is very possible today if you have access to the Internet, videos, YouTube, lots of reading materials, etc.

Reporter: One big concern many Chinese people are having about English language learning today is that they think starting learning English at very early age may compromise children's use of mother tongue. What do you think?

Rod Ellis: Yeah, I've come across the same argument in Japan. It has no basis in fact. This belief stems from a deficit model of language learning, namely that learning one language will have a negative impact on the learning of another language such as the mother tongue. But everything we know about language learning suggests in fact that it is possible to learn two (or more) languages and achieve a native-like proficiency in them at the same time. And there is plenty of research that shows this. And let me end with one other very interesting advantage of bilingualism. Research has looked at the extent to which bilinguals suffer from Alzheimer's disease in later age compared to monolinguals. What this research shows is that bilingual people can still get Alzheimer's disease, but they get it later than monolinguals. In other words, the act of learning two languages gives you a cognitive advantage by helping you to ward off something as terrible as Alzheimer's later in life.

Reporter: Task-based language teaching, or TBLT, has become an important way to improve students' communicative ability in many Asian classes. How should Chinese teachers use it effectively in their class and what might be the future challenges for TBLT?

Rod Ellis: Let me go back to what I said a moment ago. You asked me what the factors are that help to make the learning of English successful in China. I mentioned two things—firstly, motivating and lively classes and, secondly, what people do to learn outside the classroom. To my mind, TBLT addresses the first of those because it provides an opportunity for teachers to teach a language in a much more motivating, lively way than how it has been taught traditionally. Doing tasks can be fun. And so the biggest reason for task-based language teaching is perhaps its motivating force. How can we ensure that task-based language teaching is carried out effectively in China? Again, we need to recognize that the issue of how best to implement TBLT is not specific to China. It is a general issue. Anywhere where TBLT has been introduced there are issues and problems. The simple answer to your question is teacher training. And that really also takes us back to the point I made about ensuring that there are opportunities for children to learn English outside the big urban centers of China. Universities need to train teachers to teach English using TBLT. Why TBLT? Because as I have said, my model is fluency-first, accuracy-later. What TBLT does is to develop the ability to communicate. It builds confidence in using English, and that to my mind, that is what the goal should be at school level and particularly in the elementary school.

Reporter: We know you are currently a Research Professor at Curtin University in Perth, Australia. Are you still involved in teaching? How much of your work time is involved in research?

Rod Ellis: The only teaching I do for Curtin University is on an MA unit on Task-based Language Teaching for Vietnamese students in Vietnam. But I do have five PhD students whom I supervise. Otherwise I am engaged in research, including a research project on testing pragmatic competence funded by the Australian Research Council. Of course, I do some teaching in my role as Visiting Professor at Shanghai International Studies University.

Reporter: In a career spanning more than 40 years, what trends do you see for English language teaching?

Rod Ellis: I am wary of predicting trends but the most obvious development in recent years has been in electronically mediated language teaching and teacher training. As in all spheres of life, electronically mediated activity will continue to increase in both language teaching and teacher training. The closing of universities due to the coronavirus will drive this development faster. Asian countries are behind in this and need to catch up.

Reporter: As a well-known proponent of Task-Based Language Teaching (TBLT), what do you think helps differentiate TBLT from other teaching approaches?

Rod Ellis: The main difference between TBLT and other, more traditional approaches is that it takes "task" not "language" as its starting point for a language curriculum. That is, in a task-based lesson there is no prior specification of the language that will be taught and learned. The focus is on achieving the task outcome. What students learn from performing a task cannot be predicted accurately. In TBLT they learn the language continuously with learning to use it to communicate. The distinction between "knowing" and "using" disappears.

Reporter: What could teachers do to accommodate TBLT to the needs of students with low language proficiency?

Rod Ellis: I have written extensively about how to do TBLT with beginner level or low proficiency students. Clearly such students are not ready to perform speaking tasks. For this reason, teachers need to make use of input-based tasks (i. e. simple listening and reading tasks), which can get students started on learning and provide the basis for output-based tasks later. I have written an article on using input-based tasks with beginner learners in the *Journal of Language Teaching to Young Learners*. And, by the way, I'd like to encourage readers of this interview to have a look at this journal and to think about contributing to it.

Reporter: There are a few mismatches between teaching and learning traditions in China and the principles of TBLT. For example, Chinese students depend heavily on the teacher while TBLT requires students to learn independently. If you were a teacher, what strategies would you employ to help students learn independently?

Rod Ellis: It is a fallacy to characterize TBLT as "learner-centered" and requiring students to learn independently. While it is true that small group work has an important place in TBLT, not all lessons—or all parts of a lesson—need to be based on small group work. For example, input-based tasks are inevitably teacher-centered (i. e. the teacher performs these tasks with the whole class). Even information-gap speaking tasks can be performed with the whole class. What is perhaps different between TBLT and learning traditions in China is that students are not told which specific language they are supposed to learn. Traditional teaching requires intentional learning. TBLT requires incidental learning.

Reporter: With the development of communicative approach in China, many teachers think it is unnecessary for students to learn grammar. Do any other Asian countries have the same phenomenon? Do you think it's possible to learn English as a foreign language without studying grammar?

Rod Ellis: Grammar teaching and intentional grammar learning lie at the heart of most language curricula in Asian countries although educational authorities throughout Asia are trying to move away from this. The problem is that the examinations continue to be quite traditional and encourage a focus on grammar. Is it possible to learn a language without learning grammar? No, learning grammar is an essential part of language learning, but it doesn't have to be learned intentionally, it can be learned incidentally, for example through extensive reading. So, is it possible to learn a language without studying grammar? Yes, there is no need to study grammar. But in my view some intentional learning of grammar is helpful and perhaps unavoidable so long as it does not become the main way of trying to learn a language. My opinion differs from some other advocates of TBLT, who see no room for intentional grammar learning.

Reporter: How can teachers keep a balance between a focus on meaning and a focus on form during TBLT?

Rod Ellis: TBLT involves both a focus on meaning and on form. The pre-task phase of a lesson offers an opportunity for focusing on form (but vocabulary rather than grammar). The post-task phase can also involve form-focused activities. In the main task phase, which is where students perform the task, the primary focus should be achieving the task outcome and therefore on meaning. But there is also an opportunity for some focus on form during this phase—for example, when a student makes an error, the teacher can quickly correct it or, in the case of an input-based task the teacher can repeat and emphasize a key word or phrase to help students process the meaning while listening. Teachers need to be skilled in drawing students' attention to form without losing sight of the task purpose, which is to achieve the task outcome.

Reporter: Assignment/Homework is an important means by which language learning is successfully achieved. However, in the real situation many teachers assign homework to their students in a "random" manner, resulting in that practice doesn't necessarily make perfect. From the teachers' perspective, what should they do to make the assignment/homework more effective, or what principles should they follow when they design assignment/homework?

Rod Ellis: I am not sure practice ever makes perfect—at least not where language learning is concerned and probably not in any aspects of life. I think we should get rid of this glib axiom "practice makes perfect". Homework clearly has a part to play in TBLT. Class time needs to be spent on performing tasks and facilitating incidental learning. But homework offers an opportunity for intentional learning—for example, learning some of the words that figure in performing a task. Homework also offers the opportunity to rehearse tasks. For example, students could be asked to repeat a task they did in class, record it on their cellphone, play it back and listen to it, and then have another go at recording it before sending it to their teacher. Or if they recorded their performance of a task in class, they could replay it, prepare a transcript of what was said, identify the errors they and other students made, and try to correct them.

Reporter: As the general understanding of TBLT develops, the expectations on the teachers grow. Teachers who lack a systematic understanding of TBLT may end up feeling overwhelmed. If you were a teacher trainer, what would you do to help them get through the struggles?

Rod Ellis: This is really a question about the importance of teacher-training. Yes, TBLT will never thrive unless teachers receive training in how to do it and develop expertise in designing their own tasks. But for teachers who have not received training I have a suggestion. They could read my short and simple book *Introducing Task-based Language Teaching* published by Shanghai Foreign Language Education Press. Then, rather than trying to switch overnight to doing TBLT, which is not likely to work, they could experiment with the occasional task-based lesson or else set aside 10 minutes in their normal lessons to experiment with tasks.

Reporter: As an author of numerous reference books and coursebooks, do you remember your first journal publication article? If a Chinese novice researcher wants to get his/her research published in internationally recognized journals, what suggestions would you give them?

Rod Ellis: I don't have a clear recollection of my first journal article. I have a good recollection of a language course I wrote with Brian Tomlinson for use in Zambia in the 1970s. I also have a good recall of my first academic book—*Classroom Second Language Development*, published by Pergamon but probably out of print now. This was partly based on my PhD thesis. Getting published in international journals is difficult and the first thing to understand is that you must be prepared to fail and try and try again. The first article I submitted to a journal was rejected. That I do remember! If you are new to publishing, it is best to start with something concrete and practical (don't get lost in abstractions and theory) and aim for a journal that publishes articles of this kind. Also decide on the journal you are writing for before you begin to write and check that journal's guidelines before submitting an article.

Donald Freeman

Donald Freeman is a professor of education at the University of Michigan, US, where his work focuses on researching and designing ELT teacher learning at scale. He is a past TESOL president, past chair of TIRF, and a senior advisor on the ELTeach Project (National Geographic Learning), which provides online professional development to ELT public sector teachers worldwide.

Improve Teaching by Developing Professional Confidence

An Interview with Donald Freeman

Reporter: How do you define professional confidence?

Donald Freeman: I think of professional confidence more now as teaching confidence, because teaching is the core of what the teacher does as a professional. There are other things that are part of professional identity and confidence, but I'm interested in this core, which is teaching. I think of teaching confidence as having two dimensions to it: One is knowing and the other is believing. Knowing is about what a teacher needs to know. What do they need to know how to do? What do they need to know about their students in order to teach well? But all of that knowledge doesn't work unless they believe that it will work with the students that they're teaching. So believing is the other side of the coin of teaching confidence. As a teacher, believing that when I use English to organize my classroom, my students are going to understand what it is I'm asking them to do. When I give them instructions that they'll be able to do what I want them to do, and when I listen to their answers I will be able to correct them in a way that they will understand, and so on.

Reporter: How could professional confidence improve teachers' capabilities?

Donald Freeman: That's a good question. It goes back to this core of teaching confidence. We've been developing this idea over the last seven years in a large-scale research-development project in 23 different countries, one of which is China. The project, *ELTeach*, looks at what public-sector English language teachers need in order to support the improvement of their teaching. We have found that most of the concepts we rely on to improve teaching—improving general English proficiency for example—are based on what teachers can't do. These concepts are based on the idea of deficit—on what the teacher is missing and what needs to be improved. In the *ELTeach* project, we began with the question: What happens when professional development focuses on what teachers already do, on their current practices that can be made better or extended? The notion of teaching confidence builds on this central premise. Rather than saying to a teacher: You don't know how to do this and you need to learn how to do it, and then do it in your classroom, teaching confidence reverses the order of that argument. Teaching confidence says to the teacher, "Let's look at what you know how to do in the classroom, and let's look at how we can strengthen your belief that what you do will be effective and will work with your students. " So teaching confidence can be the core of professional development that is to build on what teachers know and are already doing, in order to improve and extend it. This approach is fundamentally different from most reform and professional development which is oriented toward fixing problems and remedying deficits.

Reporter: What are your suggestions on developing professional confidence?

Donald Freeman: I think English teachers in China have much in common with teachers in other countries where I've worked. There are three central issues. First, as a teacher you need to think about your students and what it is that they need to do. And when I say "need to do", I mean, what is part of their trajectory as learners? This is not simply the exams they must pass or the curriculum that you must teach them. Their learning trajectory is about where they are headed, what is it that they want to be able to do? Second, knowing that trajectory, you need to think about how you can support them in moving forward. This is believing dimension of teaching confidence we just spoke about. As a teacher, I need to believe that what I do will help my students move along the path that they need to follow. And the third issue is to have faith in what you know and what you're capable of doing. Too often, I think, in many contexts, we present teachers, as I said earlier, with the problems that they have not solved. All this deficit approach does is to reinforce a negative. To improve teaching and learning, we need to reinforce what is working and to extend and improve on it. Teachers in China—like their counterparts in most countries—know what works in their classrooms. Our job in professional development is to figure out how we can support them to extend and complexify their knowledge. As someone who works with teachers around the world, this is my goal.

Reporter: What core competencies do you think a good ESL teacher should have?

Donald Freeman: I'd give two answers. My first is that a "good" teacher needs the competencies to get the job done. I don't mean this facetiously. Competency has to be locally understood; at the "core" it involves being able to figure out what is working and what isn't in terms of your students and their learning. So I suppose the core competency is to be a good diagnostician. My second answer is that different national and transnational groups have set out definitions of teaching competencies—for example, the National Foreign Language Teachers Association in China or TESOL International have documented frameworks. These are useful in creating a common language about classroom practice. But we need to keep in mind that competency in teaching (or even language) is not something you have (or don't have), it is something you do and if you are a diagnostician, you can get better over time at doing it.

Reporter: What do you think are the common deficiencies in the professional development of English language teachers globally?

Donald Freeman: I see the problems of deficiencies as being more conceptual than implementational—these deficiencies lie in how we define what we are trying to do more than in how we are trying to do it. To give an example: in many professional development settings, English teachers' knowledge is defined in terms of their level of general proficiency, usually as documented by the CEFR. "Good" teachers are more fluent in English, the argument goes, therefore logically teachers who are less at ease in

English must be "less good." However, the problem is there is no such thing as "general proficiency"; it's an abstraction that doesn't correspond with the world. But the abstraction is used all the time to judge who is "more" or "less" fluent and, when these judgments are applied to teachers, who is "more" or "less" qualified. In daily life, we are always using language in particular circumstances and the abstraction of "general proficiency" tries to summarize or average out those diverse circumstances. Then teachers' English is measured against this fiction, and many are told they need to improve their language proficiency.

There is a second problem with using this idea of general language proficiency to evaluate English teachers' competence. While it may seem like common sense, there has not been solid research to support the idea. So the better question for professional development is what English do classroom teachers need to know in order to teach in English? It may well be the case that these teachers need (and often want to) have a better command of English to do their jobs but developing the specific English to use in this context as a classroom teacher doesn't necessarily happen efficiently or effectively in a general language course setting.

Reporter: In China, there are currently many rural English teachers who lack professional knowledge and have insufficient teaching skills. Given the relatively limited resources, what are your suggestions for the professional development of rural English teachers?

Donald Freeman: China is not the only country with an urban-rural divide in its teaching force. We did work in Vietnam for example, where a similar gap exists. We found that with professional development that focused specifically on classroom English—*English-for-teaching*—and on classroom methodology, teachers in rural areas progressed and developed confidence similar to their urban colleagues. The key was how the professional development was designed: It was not offered as courses or workshops; in fact it wasn't even in person. Instead, the teachers had access to online modules on *English-for-Teaching* and classroom methodology for a period of time (usually three months) and there was an assessment at the end of the time. The teachers could study and practice whenever they wanted, as much (or as little) as they felt they needed to master the content. Data from successive, large-scale implementations showed that many teachers in rural areas studied longer than those in urban areas in order to reach the same level on the assessment.

Reporter: A long-standing concern in the field of teacher education is how to translate teaching theories into practice. What do you think is the root cause of teachers' difficulties in translating theories into practice? How can teachers get out of this dilemma?

Donald Freeman: I hate to sound flip, but I think it's a non-problem. What we call "theory" and what we call "practice" are essentially two languages about the same thing; in our case, about English language teaching and learning. As academics, we talk theory and so do many teachers. But more classroom folks speak the language of practice. Theory as a language (or discourse) concentrates on generalization and abstraction; the intention is to be a world unto itself. Classroom practice is a different language; as a discourse it focuses on what is immediate in time and space. So while academics write and talk about motivation for example, their classroom teacher colleagues think and talk about how their third-period class of middle-schoolers are liking or not liking the lesson in the textbook on leisure activities. The American novelist Eudora Welty used to say about writing that "the general resides in the particular. " The same can be said about theory—that it resides in practice. Its generalizations are only as useful as the specific cases in which they are seen.

Reporter: As a new social presence, the Internet will be deeply integrated with all aspects of education. What do you think the "Internet plus Education" model has to say about English teacher education?

Donald Freeman: I'm not familiar with the phrase, but I guess it refers to the range of information available on the Internet, how accessible that information can be, and so how this challenges the dynamic of knowledge and skills transmission that is fundamental in most educational designs (teacher education included). The Internet changes a lot of things, but the most basic is the way we think about individual agency and engagement.

It is not that "information is power" as the saying goes; it is that the possibility that you can get information yourself that is powerful. But to be useful, getting information means that you need to be able to determine the accuracy or truth of what you are finding. The Internet shifts the balance of power in the knowledge equation—anyone with access can potentially get information and that access challenges how we think about formal education. At the same time, the shift introduces a different role for educators—it is a role of helping folks to think about what's the information they are finding.

Lixian Jin

Lixian Jin is the Chair Professor of Applied Linguistics and the Dean of Faculty of Humanities and Social Sciences at the City University of Macau after working in the UK universities for over 30 years achieving a Chair Professor in Linguistics and Intercultural Learning. Her research focuses on English language teaching, intercultural communication, speech and language therapy, cultures of learning and narrative and metaphor analyses. She has published over 200 research-based books, chapters and journal articles, including several sets of College English textbooks and teachers' books for Chinese and international learners from kindergarten to university levels as an author, translator and editor jointly produced in teams. She has been voted to become the President of the International Association of Intercultural Communication Studies in 2023−2025.

Intercultural Communication and Applied Linguistics —Extending Horizons

An Interview with Lixian Jin

Reporter: We'd like to start off on a more personal note, Prof. Jin. I would first invite you to talk about your academic and professional life highlighting how you got interested in Applied Linguistics and TESOL.

Lixian Jin: This is a long story. English was not my original career choice. I wanted to become a medical doctor. But fate has taken me on a pathway of English and then to applied linguistics and TESOL.

At school, it was not possible for me to learn English properly. During 1966 – 1976, schools were closed for long periods or open but with little teaching. What we learned, intermittently, was from an English textbook which highlighted political slogans. We had to memorise those words to pass the exam, but we did not really learn listening or speaking, reading or writing. Later, I hardly attended senior high school. I went to study traditional Chinese medicine outside school, wanting to become a barefoot doctor. Then I worked as a replacement teacher for one year at a local primary school. I taught Chinese and Maths and, somehow, taught English to the middle school year-one class attached to the primary school. A year later, I was back to Chinese herbal medicine: I was assigned to work in a traditional Chinese medicine faculty, but everything changed when I passed the first national university entrance exam in

1977 and was luckily admitted to study English literature and language at university.

So how about learning English in these circumstances? During my brief schooling and factory work time, my parents were very wise. They heard me reading English sentences with awful English pronunciation, so they found an old friend to help. He was an English teacher. I used to go to his house every Sunday morning to learn some English and the rest of the time I was supposed to do home-study alone. But mostly I was simply exhausted, because in the factory I was often required to do extended work hours (from 7 am to 9 pm, six days a week). I worked as a construction labourer to move bricks and soil for the factory building, as an assembly line worker to wrap labels on medicine bottles, as a mechanic apprentice (a very much admired job then) with which I learned how to fix some mechanical equipment, to do welding to repair high chimneys, and to design and make moulds; as a herbal-extraction worker to produce Chinese medicines for intravenous injections. Sunday was the only time to catch up on sleep or daily life. Again, I hardly had the opportunity to hear English, although the teacher specially corrected my pronunciation here and there. We hardly finished one textbook during the years of studying with him. When we heard about the chance to go to university, this English teacher and another English teacher from my middle school both encouraged me to attend the exam — for the English major. All I knew was that I wanted to study in a university: I did not care what subject it might be. By that time, my father had passed away. My mother was still suffering under the consequences of the ten-year turbulent period, so I had no one else to turn to. My mother had no income. She wanted me to keep my "good" steady-income job as a Chinese medicine factory worker. So I had to do my English revision and exam preparation secretly, outside in a street under the street-light whenever I had time.

Fortunately, I managed to pass the exam. Nevertheless, my mother was strongly against the idea for me to go to a normal university: for her, having a good factory job was the best choice. She worried about our income situation. Luckily, to allow me to go to study, my uncles agreed to support my mother's living expenses. However, when I got to university to study English, I could hardly say a word, not even to reply to greetings. It was embarrassing. At first this was a great struggle—everyone was better than I was at English. But I worked hard in class and especially out of class: I grabbed tape recordings to listen to English for as many hours a day as I could, plus reading texts, reciting passages aloud, learning vocabulary, and talking to myself even in my dreams. Once I understood some English words from the film *The Sound of Music*, I was so excited and felt proud. I have been watching this film many times since, and I still get the same feeling of contentment and satisfaction. A good classmate helped me practise my oral English: we've remained life-long friends. Another piece of luck was to have two American teachers (at that time, a handful of foreign teachers were assigned to teach English majors at only three universities in the whole Hubei Province), and the best Chinese teachers of English. They devoted their time and energy to teaching us.

After a year or so, my English had improved a lot. I won the university English-speaking contests a few times. This gave me the confidence to develop a special interest in English pronunciation. Every winter and summer holiday, I went to Beijing to join my uncles' families. They were all good at English and they supported me to study well. During those visits, I used to take notes from the limited linguistic books available in the Beijing Library. I read about the concept of clinical linguistics one day. I thought it would be wonderful if I could study clinical linguistics, then at least I could use some linguistics linked with medical sciences, since I had always wanted to become a medical doctor. By chance—or fate—years later, my first full-time job in a British university was to teach clinical linguistics to train speech and language therapists in a health and life sciences environment. For this, I had to seriously study the content before teaching it. I was well trained as an applied linguist and a linguist, but this does not mean I could teach every subject in the fast-expanding field of applied linguistics. Well, I did that job for 18 years and conducted research in clinical linguistics.

Going back to my university time in China, by graduation for my first degree, my English was considered "competent". My oral English was fluent and I was acting as an interpreter at university international meetings. My graduation dissertation on "The Problems of Wuhan People in Learning English Pronunciation", considered the best BA dissertation, was published as a journal article in the 1980s after going through many reviews and some special approval by a well-known professor in linguistics (I was considered too junior to be allowed to publish an academic paper). So, this was my first academic publication. I was appointed to stay on as a university English teacher, specialising in English Phonetics and Phonology. I taught there for nearly 5 years before I left to do my MA and PhD in Applied Linguistics and Education in the UK, with the first non-government scholarship funded by several British educational foundations (in itself another long story).

Reporter: You have done quite a lot of research on intercultural communication vis-à-vis TESOL. Can you tell us a little about what got you interested in these areas, what your research has found and how your findings can help teachers and learners?

Lixian Jin: To me, intercultural communication (IC) is a vital part of learning a foreign language. Students need to have the curiosity, patience and empathy to engage with a range of cultures. These qualities are worth developing for themselves; additionally, many students will be future professional language users. Cultures are parts of languages and languages are part of cultures. Learners need to appreciate through good examples in different contexts how different communities of English users (whether as a first, second or other language, or as a lingua franca or global English) not only have different styles of communication, but often different ways of conveying meaning, because their communication for some topics is based on different assumptions and so their expression in discourse might be hard for others to follow to get the main meaning without some knowledge and feeling about the people and their language use. Cultures create meanings but meanings also create cultures.

When I was searching for a worthwhile research focus for PhD, I realised that Chinese research students at that time in Britain were suffering a lot socially, psychologically and academically, even though they were from elite academic groups in China. They were confident that they were competent, but it seemed that they were not treated with respect by other students or staff. At the same time, British supervisors also commented that Chinese students were the most hard-working, intelligent, and self-sacrificing students they had ever met. These supervisors wanted to help Chinese students achieve more, but they did not know how the students could get into relevant "Western" ways of thinking for their research or writing. So, for my PhD I decided to explore these intercultural academic gaps between the Chinese research students and their British supervisors.

My research findings have shown that there are different emphases in ways of learning, teaching and research: these are perceived by people coming from different social, psychological and academic backgrounds and inherited learning methods and beliefs. This might lead to different preferences in learning or teaching, e. g. tendencies to ask (or not ask) questions in discussion. Sometimes what is appreciated or valued by some academics (or other learners) may not seem important or relevant to other academics (or other learners). This is partly influenced by their cultural beliefs: about what a good student or teacher is, what is considered good learning or research, or how they should interact in academic settings. For instance, to ask a question of a superior (a teacher or supervisor) may be perceived as impolite or inappropriate in academic settings by some Chinese students. They might think that the act of asking a question is itself a challenge, so they would not dare to ask questions with their supervisors, even if they see alternatives or have doubts about the ideas presented. They may be reluctant to ask any questions at all. I refer to this preferred academic behaviour as cultures of learning, because ways of learning vary, culturally, around the world. It means IC includes cultural learning, of course, but it also includes learning about other's learning.

So Intercultural Communication (IC), as a large field, includes the interaction in language learning and teaching. I mean, language learning depends on cultures of learning and cultures of communication and these can be surprisingly different around the world or even within one country or one discipline of a university. How students learn and how teachers teach depend partly on their upbringing and socialization, education and training, on what they think language is, and how they believe people should teach and learn. For example, in one case, textbooks have questions and teachers ask these or make their own questions based on the book; students may give answers and sometimes everyone expects a single answer to each question: this answer is right or wrong (often confirmed as such by the answer given in the textbook or teacher's book). In this case, good learning means correctly answering questions, and the questions are often about something already taught. In effect, this particular learning means reading and listening in order to spot and remember answers to upcoming questions (e. g. for a test or an exam). This could be an overlooked IC issue.

In other cultures, there are cases where teachers (and students) perceive that many questions have a range of answers, so several different answers might be sought and discussed. In such cultures, educationally, teachers believe that students (not only teachers) ought to be asking questions: asking is a major way of learning. So, they develop techniques to encourage learners to ask and to be creative with thinking about their own questions, and not only to recall answers to teacher-or-book questions. Teachers in this second case are disappointed if students don't have questions: they think good teaching leads to learner questions, and that learner questions lead to accelerated, deeper or more emotionally-engaged learning. Good learners here should be eager to ask. In this kind of contrast, perhaps students in the first case don't ask, because the questions all come from the teacher or textbook. They are not used to asking. If a teacher does say, "Any questions?" the students believe this is just a routine formula and it is not serious; or they don't want to interrupt the teacher; or they might think that to ask a question shows ignorance (rather than eagerness for knowledge and interaction) and perhaps they are afraid of negative comments from their peers.

So, this question of questions can be one small part of different cultures of learning. The concept of cultures of learning does not necessarily mean it has to do with learning styles or other aspects of cultures of learning between countries/communities, but it can be within one cultural community of a country, or these can be experienced through reflection even within individuals during their journeys of learning. Internationally, these cultures involve ways of developing intercultural communication in the actual moment-to-moment teaching and learning. So, IC is not only something outside the classroom, or only something for preparation for a future profession using English: it's in the classroom process and in daily interaction between teacher and class or between different groups of students, as well as communicating in English outside class. If the classroom process does not involve practical IC and intercultural thinking in some way (e. g. developing repertoires of ways of asking in intercultural situations in role playing), it is less likely to be effective in the real world.

Reporter: In your keynote presentation *Internationalisation in HE*, you have mentioned that intercultural communication might be carried out within a framework of internationalisation. Could you elaborate on it?

Lixian Jin: Internationalisation has been perceived as essential in business contexts and later in education since receiving international students and having international collaboration have become a part of the rating mechanism for league tables in university ranking. But what I have been arguing is that this internationalisation is not just a matter of student numbers, or university income, or points for reputation and status. More significantly, there should be substantial support for mind-and-heart internationalisation in business or education. It means developing a profound sense of "planetization", a deep awareness that all nations and peoples are all on the same planet, interacting with each other and within the same global environment. It means international and local students learn culturally from each other. It means teachers as professionals (and students as future professionals) need to develop intercultural communication competence (ICC) in order to achieve a real sense of internationalisation, cognitively, emotionally, socially and culturally. When international students (and staff) are in a university, this does not necessarily mean the university is "internationalised" unless true intercultural communication takes place to bring all partners (i. e. academic, administrative, technical staff and students) up to a level in which they understand, empathize and appreciate each other, not only in their work roles but as people on one planet.

I have brought in the argument of having awareness of cultures of learning and teaching. This has the aim to help make university a synergetic place, in which both staff and students treat each other with openness and curiosity about each other's repertoires of learning and teaching styles to make education truly international in curriculum, in thinking, in practice. This helps to create future professionals ready to serve the global workplace. People may argue that international students go to study in a British university, because they want to be educated by British ways. But what are British ways? Historically, and now, British businesses and society generally have been absorbing many resources internationally. In a reverse argument, staff in a British university might not learn all the styles of learning from all international students (and of course so many other aspects of cultures and worldviews). But the aim is not for one person to learn all styles of teaching and learning (and about all cultures). This is impossible in reality. But it is possible for staff and students to learn some principles for being aware of various preferred styles of teaching and learning, more importantly, to establish an open channel to explicitly explain their own thoughts about teaching and learning, while learning from and with others. Even if each participant insists on their own preferred ways of teaching and learning (which may be considered as their right), they would provide explicit information and insight so that other participants would make informed choices of learning and teaching. This strand of internationalisation is important because it suggests a teaching-and-learning process, a stance of investigation and imagination, as central to the international purpose and improved functioning of a university.

Reporter: What does intercultural communication mean? What role should intercultural communication play in TESOL? How should English language teachers promote EFL/ESL learners' intercultural competence?

Lixian Jin: I have answered parts of these questions earlier. I would like to focus on the ways for ELT teachers to promote intercultural communication competence (ICC) in their teaching to EFL/ESL learners. There are many ways to teach and learn IC. Here I only mention three points which we often apply in our teaching. First, teachers will help students understand the broad concepts of what culture is, of what cultures do, and how cultures make and communicate meanings. This is not necessarily about different national cultures, but it could relate to students themselves, e. g. coming from different parts of the country or different cities or family backgrounds. Culture is partly about people's expectations, attitudes, preferences and perceptions which influence their thoughts and chosen behaviour. So, when we interact with people, we need to be open to others' views, to be aware of alternatives when we interpret their behaviour and learn to think from others' perspectives, while postponing judgements. Secondly, teachers can be good examples of performing ICC in their teaching by guiding students to explore IC cases with thoughtfulness and empathy. Thirdly, teachers can raise students' sensitivity, curiosity, openness and awareness of intercultural issues for effective communication purposes. For example, in my teaching, I ask students to create their own lists of "key IC ideas" or "rules" by producing their own acrostic to remind themselves of IC in their daily action. For instance, some students in a group made an acrostic of RESPECT:

Recognize differences between individuals;

Evaluate everyone's behaviours without discrimination;

Smile is a good beginning to show your kindness;

People should think about issues from each other's point of view;

Explanation is a way to solve misunderstanding and conflict;

Controlling your emotion is necessary in communication;

Try to be patient when facing difficulties.

Students work through IC theories in discussion. They read other's groupwork to internalise their own (and other's) understanding and create their own ways to think and behave in IC.

Reporter: At De Montfort University (DMU), UK, you developed one of the few UK Master's programmes on Intercultural Business Communication and established an intercultural research centre for learning and communication. Can you share with us the interesting/challenging bits of this experience?

Lixian Jin: Around 2009 I initiated this innovative programme. There were just two similar programmes in the UK then. People did not know what this programme was about and why "intercultural" was part of the degree title. I had to convince different university committees that "intercultural communication competence" can be decisive for success in a business negotiation. We need to educate students who are able to handle intercultural business with communication competence, intercultural understanding, integrated with business or professional knowledge. I got some funding from the UK Prime Minister's Initiative fund, the findings demonstrate how business needs a trained workforce with ICC for their globalized work contexts.

I also faced a problem of where to locate this programme, since it involved staff from three faculties: Humanities, Business and Health and Life Sciences (where I was affiliated with). I wanted to locate it in my faculty, because the research and teaching could also link with speech and language therapy and other health professions trained in the faculty. In the end, the university agreed with my reasons that this programme would remain in the Life and Health Sciences Faculty, so I set up a teaching and research centre called Centre for Intercultural Research in Communication and Learning (CIRCL). Staff were from different faculties to be truly intercultural and interdisciplinary. Intercultural problems were solved through intercultural communication and action. The programme included many international students and many visiting scholars from China participated.

Reporter: In your current new position as Dean of Faculty of Humanities and Social Sciences in the City University of Macau (Macau SAR, China), do you need to develop a similar master's or doctoral programme in the broad area of Applied Linguistics? What are your visions for the new programme(s) at your current institution? What difficulties do you need to address?

Lixian Jin: In my first month of arriving at the City University of Macau in August 2021, I led a group of staff members to work on proposals to establish Applied Linguistics programmes for BA, MA and PhD levels. We worked day-and-night for 20 days to produce over 50 documents for this application. There is currently no Applied Linguistics programme in Macau. It is timely to establish programmes at all levels to support the infrastructure of future workforces in Macau and the Greater Bay Area.

The Applied Linguistics degrees include different strands: for the BA, two strands are proposed which are on Language in Education for those who would like to develop their future career in ELT and on Intercultural Communication for those who would like to use IC for their professional development; for the MA, four strands are planned: TESOL, TCSOL (Teaching Chinese to Speakers of Other Languages), Teaching Languages to Young Learners, and IC. The main consideration is that these specialities are currently not available in education in Macau and the graduates would be able to fulfil the language needs locally, as well as in other areas of China (including the Greater Bay area) and elsewhere. As applied linguists, we aim to solve problems in education and other fields. In order to achieve the goals of meeting the educational and professional needs, we have designed work placements in all our degree programmes. Of course, this can be challenging: we are considering suitable work placement locations so that our students will benefit from applying their knowledge and skills into real world settings. We are also facing some difficulties to expand our staff expertise. Currently we are recruiting a large number of academics from lecturer to professor levels. We welcome talented academics to join us for the mission of providing good education for Macau and the Greater Bay Area.

Reporter: There are 60 million Chinese primary school children (based on China Education 2013) learning English at the age of nine or even younger (e. g. , seven). To what extent is this popular TESOL-related belief true that "the earlier, the better"?

Lixian Jin: This is a complicated question. People may know that the "critical period hypothesis" has influenced some decisions about early starting for learning English. Some primary schools in China start the teaching of English from Year 1 and some choose to start from Year 3. There are several issues we need to consider for teaching English to young learners (EYL).

Firstly, this is not simply a question of timing the starting age for learning English; how we teach young learners is a more important issue. This is a reason that the City

University of Macau would like to develop this strand of teaching EYL in order to produce specialists who can handle this teaching more effectively as teachers. The learners are young and usually keen to learn any knowledge and skills; if we teach them as if they are adult learners (e. g. focusing on testing them, or forcing them to learn grammar rules, or mainly memorizing) we will kill their enthusiasm for learning. I have conducted a series of funded projects investigating motivations of English learning from kindergarten to university students in China. A major finding shows children need to be motivated to learn according to their emotional, intellectual and cognitive development, with a good support in social, psychological and educational provision. Children are aware of different difficulty levels in learning, but learning needs to be scaffolded so that they can use their own learning pace and readiness to progress. Teachers pay attention to individual needs, so they need to use multiple techniques fitting with children's developmental stages in learning.

Secondly, successful language learning for EYL relies on a positive linguistic environment. In international schools in China, where English could be the medium of teaching, these children would have a wider and richer exposure to English. In state schools, where children's English learning may be restricted to a couple of hours per week, this provides relatively little input to their learning. If they do not have other sources of English in their learning environment, it would be hard for them to acquire language skills. Thus, the best option is to nurture and sustain their interest in English through engaging activities and let them develop more rapidly when they are ready; meanwhile for EYL, schools can provide many short out-of-class activities and things-to-do-at-home in English (with support, parents or grandparents might be involved). Our research shows young learners are particularly keen when they could learn English together with their parents, as a rewarding time to spend with their parents.

Thirdly, teachers of English need to have regular professional training and development. In China, quite a number of provinces provide annual training plans for English teachers to update their knowledge and techniques for teaching EYL. At the same time, it may be informative and insightful for English teachers to learn from teachers of other disciplines (e. g. from teachers of Chinese) or learn from observing and collaborating in teaching styles from other levels of education, e. g. university teachers observe and collaborate with senior high school teachers in order to understand students coming from there to university level; Junior high school teachers may observe and work with primary school teachers, and primary school teachers of EYL may link with kindergarten teaching to understand how children develop their learning, and become familiar with different teaching styles from different educational stages.

Reporter: When your research subjects include very young learners, did you have any difficulties in soliciting the cooperation of your research subjects? How did you overcome these difficulties?

Lixian Jin: This is a useful question to many researchers who are interested in young learners, not just for EYL. We have used a few strategies to help with data collection and analysis:

- provide as natural environment as possible as our data collection settings (in a familiar setting, with known adults, in a non-testing situation).
- collect data through playing with children (using games with toys, activities with objects, colours, picture books, etc.) and their own teachers can be research partners.
- let them get to know trained researchers in a relaxing environment (engage with children in classroom routines, before any research activities).
- model some examples by giving examples to clarify what to do, or what the activity is, maybe in several steps (particularly when using elicited metaphor analysis, which asks children to give an example of a comparison between a concrete object, e. g. "an apple", to represent their attitudes towards an abstract idea or activity, as well as asking for their reasons of using this comparison to get children's insight on a matter).
- use children's way of talking at their cognitive level to interact with them (not being patronizing or "too-teacherly", but showing that what children say or do is important, interesting and worth attention).

Of course, as research procedures, all of this has to go through ethical consideration and appropriate approval. In our cases, parents and teachers (and children) were reasonably aware of our research procedures and methods with their formal consent; often we gave general comments and feedback about the results. This is wide-ranging teamwork: we had prior consultation with kindergarten and primary school teachers, and specialist teacher-trainers. They provided valuable advice on what props and realia to use in each kindergarten or school, including about suitable time-periods for activities.

Reporter: There is an emerging research theme that examines the process and outcomes of learning of a foreign language (e. g. English) at a later stage in life (e. g. after retirement). Based on your research concerning older EFL/ESL learners, can you please share with us the takeaways?

Lixian Jin: Yes, this life-long learning is a significant development. It shows how it is never too late to learn a foreign language. One study I can share with you was completed by my past PhD student, Dr. Yanchuan Geng. His research focuses on the main reasons which motivate older learners of English in China (referring to those aged 50 and above). In contrast to other learners who may get obvious educational achievement or cognitive and linguistic improvement, one key finding from this study is the positive affective gain from learning English. This could be due to several reasons: a feeling of making up for lost opportunities in their youth when they did not have time or the chance to learn English; or they really enjoy communicating in English with their grandchildren who are learning English or leaving for study abroad; or they feel it is useful and convenient to use English in their international travel. Emotionally, they expand their life with feelings of gaining dignity, pride, happiness, enjoyment and satisfaction.

When we study this group of learners, who are sophisticated and well-experienced, we should not have fixed ways of research thinking to only use standard research methods (like questionnaire surveys or question-answer interviews). This may lead to ordinary findings because it asks standard questions. This study used elicited metaphor analysis in addition to traditional methods. This use of more innovative methods helps to dig deeper into understanding our participants. We need to treat them as valued partners and establish heart-to-heart conversations with them. Exploring their ideas and experiences through metaphors is one way.

Reporter: You have a vast teaching, research and administrative experience spanning your academic life. How compatible do you find these different roles and do you think whether language teachers should get engaged in research and administration as well as teaching?

Lixian Jin: Fundamentally, I am both a researcher and a teacher like many colleagues in education. These make my life engaging and exciting, and energetic: I gain strength and rewards from them. A researcher and a teacher should be a good leader, because we are leading students or colleagues as a part of our jobs. Different people may have different styles for leadership and management. My styles may reflect in how I do research: that is, to try to be open, transparent and fair in dealing with matters, showing respect to others and being willing to listen to others' views and advice. However, at the same time I should be firm and effective to make management decisions, be supportive when others are in need, and be responsive and responsible for any apparent errors made. In the UK, university academic staff are likely given all three roles: teaching, research and administration. All three roles are part of their challenging job. The job gives us a chance to be trained and practise our administrative capabilities. This is not necessarily a negative thing. We are all leaders in one way or another: in university, as elsewhere, everyone is a learner, everyone is a teacher, everyone is a leader in some ways. It seems positive to recognize these qualities and help to develop them in others.

Deborah Short

Deborah Short directs academic language research & training and provides professional development on academic literacy, content-based English, and sheltered instruction worldwide. She has directed research projects related to English learner education, co-developed the SIOP Model, and was a lead writer for *The 6 Principles* book. She was TESOL's President-Elect(2019—2020).

The 6 Principles for Teaching of English Learners

An Interview with Dr. Deborah Short

Reporter: With China being an increasingly important player in the field of English language education, are there any experience or theories learned from here that can be applied globally?

Deborah Short: China is a very important venue for English language education. And I think we have a lot to learn from the way English language teaching is being rolled out in such a large country where so many people are trying to learn English. I think one of the main benefits of learning English in China is the way technology is playing a role in helping people learn the language and providing a number of different resources for them to do so. It allows some independence of learning, and it allows some blended situations where people can learn online part of the time, but they can also study with a teacher in a face-to-face environment. I think we also gain insights from the fact that motivation is very high in China to learn English, and that always helps when you're trying to acquire a new language. Others around the world may want to enhance motivation and find other incentives to promote their students' language skills. In addition, China has been working on developing specialized curricula that suit their learners and also apply to the country's future needs. So they have new materials, for example, that address interests of the Chinese people who are learning English. These are very valuable tools and help the acquisition process.

Reporter: Could such curriculum developed here be used outside China?

Deborah Short: I think certain aspects of the curriculum could certainly be used outside China. And they might be modified. If some of the authentic texts are more China-specific, for example, focusing on a regional habitat or a period of Chinese history, others outside China might choose a reading that is more suited to their country or to the needs of their learners. They might have to present different vocabulary, but they could build background knowledge and teach the same reading skill or strategy using activities like those in the Chinese curriculum with the new texts. I think it's very important that we know why people are studying English and then choose the appropriate materials and design suitable lessons for their particular goals. Other ideas in the curricula being developed here can be applied to other settings, such as how to use technology and audio and video recordings as tools for language learning.

Reporter: With foreign language learning going into smaller cities, rural areas, or underdeveloped areas in China, do you think there will be more challenges or opportunities in the field?

Deborah Short: In China, there is a lot of language learning going on throughout the country and often this occurs in rural areas or smaller cities. So there are some challenges that those environments pose. For example, there may be fewer resources. There may be not as many materials, such as supplemental texts at various reading ability levels, to let teachers differentiate instruction. Perhaps there aren't as many trained teachers as needed to teach English to the students who are learning it. But that doesn't mean those challenges don't also provide opportunities. With the growth of English learning through online education, an instructor or program administrator has a way to reach some of those rural communities or the smaller cities. The opportunity to engage with authentic materials and proficient speakers through the technological advances that we have, that is a way that more and more people can learn English.

Reporter: What are the latest developments on the application of the six core principles in other parts of the world?

Deborah Short: In 2018, TESOL published the first book in the Six Principles

Initiative, *The 6 Principles for Exemplary Teaching of English Learners*. This book focused on primary and secondary education in the United States. But we have expanded the work, and there are now three more books: one that was published in 2019, one that came out in 2020, and the latest one in 2021. These are *The 6 Principles for Adult Education and Workforce Development*, *The 6 Principles for Academic and Specific Purposes*, and *The 6 Principles for Young Learners in a Multilingual World*. All four of these books offer an opportunity to spread the 6 principles around the world. And we know that they are being used in a number of different places. For example, in a number of universities, educators are using the 6 principles not only to design their lessons but to develop curriculum and work with colleagues in their departments. If they have students who are studying to be teachers of English, then they are learning how to use the 6 principles as they plan for their own classrooms. Or if they have students who are going to be using English in their professional lives, the teachers are using the 6 principles to make sure that the lessons that they deliver to these students are of the highest standard.

Reporter: How can Chinese teachers implement the 6 principles in strategic ways?

Deborah Short: Chinese teachers have ample opportunity to implement the 6 principles in strategic ways, but they might choose to develop their skills in addressing all of the 6 principles over time. It's not something that they will be able to necessarily implement right away. But they can begin with one principle and add another principle in a cumulative fashion, so that they keep adding to their repertoire of exemplary classroom practices.

First, they want to think about the purpose for which students are learning English, and the conditions in their classrooms for promoting language learning. I think what we find in China is that many people are motivated to learn English, so that helps the teachers when it comes to motivating their students in the classroom. As they do this, they have to think about the resources that they have available in the curriculum that they are using to teach English to their learners. They might make sure that they have authentic materials that demonstrate language use for real communication, such as books, stories, articles, and audio recordings. They need supports for students too like anchor charts, vocabulary walls, and visuals. I think one of the most important things to do next is to make sure that the lessons are meaningful. One key way to do that is to integrate content learning, reading, writing, and discussing different subject area topics with their English language learning.

Reporter: We know that TESOL International Association has defined the six principles for ELT and that you are one of the authors of *The 6 Principles*. Are these principles intended to be universal guidelines for English teachers?

Deborah Short: TESOL International Association is dedicated to improving the quality of English language teaching around the world and the 6 principles serve as a foundation for this. They explicate a core set of guidelines for the exemplary teaching and learning of English as a new language. The 6 principles are applicable for any school level and in any context. So teachers in China who provide English as a Foreign Language instruction to young learners, content-based English or CLIL courses to secondary students, English-medium instruction in a subject-specific course at the university level, or English for business or healthcare to adult professionals can all use the 6 principles for effective lesson planning and delivery.

The 6 principles are based on decades of research and practice in second language learning and in instructional and assessment design. They are illustrated with many teaching techniques, classroom tips, checklists, and feedback and assessment ideas. Educators can use them to make informed instructional and assessment decisions, identify strategies to promote bi/multilingualism, and set up beneficial conditions for learning in their classes. As they plan lessons or develop curricula, we want them to consider their learners first, so lessons have clear objectives and engaging tasks that help students use the new language in authentic ways. We hope that the 6 principles become a staple in teacher education and professional development. All teachers need to know how to provide high-quality instruction to English learners.

Reporter: What kind of knowledge and skills should English teachers in

China acquire in order to successfully implement the 6 principles? What do the 6 principles tell us about teacher development?

Deborah Short: As individuals study to become English language teachers, they will likely learn a wide variety of pedagogical practices and study research on second language acquisition. They will be exposed to strategies to tap into student assets and to share cultural knowledge about places and contexts where English is widely used. They will also learn about the elements of English—vocabulary, grammar, sentence structures, discourse patterns, and suggested sequences for teaching reading, writing, listening and speaking skills. *The 6 Principles for Exemplary Teaching and Learning* can be the framework for that type of teacher training, whether it happens in a university preservice program, during graduate studies, or as part of in-service professional development.

In general teachers have to "know their learners" in terms of their proficiency in English and in their home language, their educational backgrounds, and their interests, talents, and aspirations. That knowledge is central to high quality lesson planning. From that base, teachers can determine what topics and lesson objectives might pique their interest and inspire them to advance their language skills, what supports students might need to scaffold their language development or make input comprehensible, what activities and tasks will support their growing language use, and what type of feedback to provide when they practice English.

The four books describing the 6 principles in different contexts offer teachers a wealth of information and activities that will enable them to design and deliver English lessons for the 21st century; ones that will help students acquire communication skills so they can interact with diverse audiences in global environments. The books, however, are not the only source for teacher development. Principle 6 is "Engage and Collaborate within a Community of Practice." It encourages teachers to not only continue their own professional learning but to join together with colleagues to discuss and reflect on practice, share ideas and insights, co-plan lessons, analyze student data, and act as a resource to one another. By supporting each other, teachers can become better implementers of effective instruction and in turn can lead their students to language learning success.

Peter Skehan

Peter Skehan is an Honorary Research Fellow at Birkbeck College, University of London. He has previously taught at universities in the UK, New Zealand, etc. He is interested in task-based approaches to second language performance, as well as language aptitude.

Task-Based Language Teaching in China

An Interview with Peter Skehan

Reporter: Compared to other approaches, what advantages does the task-based approach have?

Peter Skehan: I think the major advantage that a task-based approach has is that it focuses on developing communicative ability. Although it takes language and grammar seriously, what it really tries to do is to show people how they can be effective in actual language use. I think one of the advantages that it has is that a task-based approach is nicely connected with a lot of research. There are other approaches which really have been proposed and have been the basis for lots of books. They're not really based on any solid amount of research. I think in the task-based approach, there are many people who are interested in teaching and learning but who are researchers, and also teachers themselves can become researchers or suggest what could be done by researchers. And I think that's an important strength to provide a foundation for the sorts of things that happen in the task-based approach.

Reporter: How do you think we could apply a task-based approach to English teaching in China?

Peter Skehan: I think that's a very difficult question, because although I think there are good things about a task-based approach, there are also ways in which a task-based approach is more difficult to put into practice, because I think it makes more demands upon the teacher. But, let's assume that those demands can be met. Then I think the key issues are going to involve effective materials for the use of tasks, to support tasks, and to anticipate something we might get onto in the moment, materials which can help at all stages of using tasks, that's to say, before, during and after the task itself. So I think, two key features that are needed are teachers who are knowledgeable, enthusiastic and effective in using tasks, and second, lots of effective materials. And perhaps I can add a third, that is, effective assessment methods which fit in with what a task-based approach tries to do. Because even if there is wonderful task-based teaching, if the nature of testing works against what happens with tasks, it's going to create difficulties for the way in which the tasks will actually be put into practice.

Reporter: You mention that more things have to be done during the post-task phase. Why do you think so? And what can teachers potentially do?

Peter Skehan: I think it goes to the heart of aspects of the task-based approach. Because in traditional language teaching, the teacher selects the language which will be taught, and the learners have to learn what has been chosen by somebody else, not necessarily what they themselves are ready to learn. In using a task-based approach, I think, what a task can do is to show what a language learner needs, what a language learner is ready to learn. The task, in other words, makes salient what the important challenges are for a learner. So the task shows what needs to be done from the learner's point of view. Then that's what has to be focused on at the post-task stage—what has been made salient by the task, through errors which are noticed, or through gaps which are revealed by what is required in the task. That's difficult for the teacher, because the teacher has to be ready to respond to something the teacher may not be expecting. Of course, a teacher can try to guess, and usually will be right, but not always. And so at the post-task stage, the teacher has to be ready to do real teaching, but teaching about something that has been shown to be important by the learners themselves. And there might be a lot of things that could be done: traditional teaching at this point based on what has emerged in the task, or even practice activities based on the task problems, or giving learners more input to look at or to listen to, again relevant to the task which has just been done. It is all a response to the language that has been shown to be important in the actual task.

Reporter: With China being an increasingly important player in the field of English language education, are there any experience or theories learned from here that can be applied globally?

Peter Skehan: Well, that's a difficult question for me, because I'm an outsider, and I don't know enough. But even so, I think, within China, you have the issue that there's enormous variation in the contexts for English teaching. And so what is learned in China about being able to deliver English language teaching in many different places could be very useful throughout the world. Because there's a danger, I think, if you think of what might be called Western approaches which make assumptions about the nature of classrooms and the teacher training and all that sort of thing, it may be difficult to export such Western approaches to many areas in the world. The Chinese experience might be more typical, and easier to generalize from. There might also be the opportunity within a Chinese approach, perhaps to be more concerned to integrate something like citizenship within language teaching. And that would be a distinctive contribution.

Reporter: Aside from the growing size of the market of foreign language teaching, what other changes have you seen from China?

Peter Skehan: Again, I'm not sure I am the person who knows most here at all. But I think one thing I would mention that's very important, and that is technology. Maybe in China, you take this for granted. But when I come to China, I'm always very impressed by how technologically advanced things are. And it seems to me, one of the areas for development in language teaching in the world is the fact that we now have amazing opportunities for exposure to language, connection with native speakers of various languages, massive amounts of input, reading and listening. And these effectively are coming because of advances in technology, and I think China could well be a major developer in that respect.

Reporter: With foreign language teaching going into smaller cities and rural areas in China, do you think there will be more challenges and opportunities for teachers?

Peter Skehan: Well, indeed, I think there will. Again, visiting China, I am very struck by the amazing development in certain areas of China, perhaps more towards the East and towards the South. And so in these areas, I think there is a more natural connection between teacher training institutions, universities and teachers. But there are many other areas within China where it's more difficult to train teachers in sufficient numbers to make an impact in English language teaching. And I think if there is going to be a solution to this difficult problem, it's got to involve technology. Because technology in many ways can be a very substitute for the more difficult learning situations in certain parts of China.

Reporter: What impact do you think on-line English teaching will have on teachers' task setting? Or how would the tasks in an online classroom differ from those in a traditional offline classroom?

Peter Skehan: Being able to use tasks inside a classroom with the teacher's opportunity to observe, and for different students to work together "live" is going to be one's first choice. But we are also fortunate that there are on-line opportunities for interaction, and we need to learn how to exploit them. One factor is going to be that the on-line resources that are available are considerable, and we can try to build into tasks the need to find good resources on the Internet that can be used within the task. So it may be, first of all, that tasks need to be designed to push students to find useful written or audio material online. This changes the teacher's role, since they have to do the research to make sure their students don't waste time with unhelpful or unsuitable resources. (The Internet contains 90% rubbish, and 10% really good material, so guidance is necessary!) So maybe there is a slight re-orientation here to tasks which depend more on reading and writing skills. Approaching tasks in this way can be good to find useful language material. It can also be good as life training, as students learn how to find good material and ignore the rubbish.

We do, though, want students to develop oral-aural skills, and maybe that is a little tricky. But again, technology does provide some help. I should apologise first of all for not being familiar with what can be done in China, and I will look at it through UK possibilities. In this case, things like WhatsApp (or WeChat?) would enable conversations to take place, and so all sorts of tasks that one could do in a classroom can also be done through electronic connections. There are even the advantages that other resources then become available—recording the interaction, for example, or even transcribing it (or machine translating it). Let people get on with these (relatively new) possibilities and they may work quite well and enable satisfactory interaction. (Remember as well that the two languages in the world that people most want to learn are English and Mandarin, and so it may be possible to set up links with schools in English-speaking countries, and engineer interesting native speaker - nonnative speaker interactions for your students.)

Of course, though, there is not the same level of control and monitoring over what is going on, and this needs to be reflected in task design. This may need more careful preparation and goal setting. Maybe there is a need to pilot tasks with a small number of typical pupils to see if they work in this new setting, and to see if things can be learned from the piloting that could lead to modification to improve the way tasks work. If you take into account that if particular tasks are successful, they can be used again next year, with new students, such piloting might be well worth doing. In class, if something isn't clear, the teacher can deal with it immediately. Using on-line communication is not so forgiving, and that's why some piloting or greater attention to task design might be necessary. Perhaps one final thing I will say about this is that one should avoid being over-complicated in working with tasks online. Maybe the tasks shouldn't be too elaborate, and maybe also, the numbers of students doing a task together should be more limited—pairs even, rather than threes or groups. Making things over-complicated might undermine the way the tasks can be effective.

In an answer to one of the earlier questions, I talk about the importance of the post-task stage, and I would like to return to that, now in relation to on-line teaching. I think there are even more reasons to pay attention to the post-task stage when we have on-line teaching. Once again, the main point is not to treat the task performance as the end of the story, and to think that the task is all there is to worry about. In some ways, it should be just the beginning. Or to put this another way, things need to happen after the task, and students need to know that these things are going to happen. With on-line interactions, there is even more of a danger that, if a task gets interesting, learners may be tempted to use Chinese! So a first aspect of post-task activity is that learners' actual task performance needs to be recorded, and they need to know that this performance may be looked at, so if they are speaking Chinese, they will be revealed not to have done the task properly! They will have to realise that they need to engage with the task, and do it in English (if that is the language being learned). But a second reason why the post-task is important is that this later stage should be a task in itself, but one that is a development of the earlier task stage. In other words, good tasks for this context are ones where there is scope for development of ideas, or language. So, if the task was to agree about something, such as the advice to the writers of letters sent into an Agony Aunt in a magazine, the post-task could be their designing a poster which organizes and presents their arguments and justifications. In this way, they "own" the task, and make it their own. They are also pushed to produce written language which is available for others to look at, and maybe comment upon. This makes the stakes a little higher, and the focus, even though this is a real task, becomes more on the actual language form that is used. A pair who produce such a poster could then be asked to defend it against other students in the class, thus building in the scope for repetition, a highly desirable feature of task implementation. Finally, of course, the language which can be looked at after the task is excellent material for the teacher to design personalized instruction which feeds off exactly the aspects of language that the students, in their task performances, need work. In this way, the teacher can start from exactly where the learners most need help.

Reporter: You have a study on developing a task-based approach to assessment in Asian context. What principles do you think English teachers in

China should follow when setting task-based tests?

Peter Skehan: A first issue is to consider, in general, the types of assessment that there are. Testers distinguish between summative assessment (the sort used by the school, or even the Ministry of Education at the end of the year, and which will be used for wider ranging decision making) and formative assessment (the sort which asks whether individual students have learned particular things, and where the answer will feed back into more teaching). The first is likely to be done for institutional reasons, while the latter is likely to be focused on an actual classroom or individual, and the results used immediately. There is a tension between these two forms of assessment everywhere, and China is no exception to this. The tension is typically that summative assessment emphasizes things you can easily count and which are claimed to be objective (and so school principals or Ministers use them) while formative assessment is more connected to the teaching methods used in the classroom (and is used by class teachers and the actual students). With task based approaches there is a problem if the task-based approach from the classroom is not matched by the approach to summative and national assessment (and usually this is exactly the case). Teachers everywhere have to find ways of squaring this circle, and this is very, very difficult.

I'll make the assumption for present purposes that the focus is on a more formative, classroom-based type of assessment. The first problem is that, however good a classroom teacher's ideas are for such assessment linked to a task-based approach, they will need to align in some way with the broader summative assessment situation. Otherwise there will be complaints that the sort of assessment done by a teacher does not help learners to handle the summative (and very important) assessment that they will face. I'll focus here on the sort of work done by a PhD student of mine, Luo Shaoqian, at BNU. She tried to develop methods of helping teachers devise assessments which (a) conformed to the National Curriculum at that time, and (b) were genuinely task-based in their approach, not least because they were interesting to the students, and worth doing. She took some of the National Curriculum themes and then tried to develop tasks for each theme at three levels of difficulty. (Testers love difficulty levels.) Then she tried these out with students, and teachers, and got the teachers to rate the difficulty level. She devised a rating scale to help teachers do this and it was successful, and her work is worth reading. It shows how tasks which teachers would recognize as tasks can also fit into the way testers think about things.

One other point I would make is that, since assessment is so difficult, a good approach would be for teachers to work collaboratively. Not only do teachers have to devise test-tasks which fit into the curriculum context, they also have to check that the test-tasks work, e. g. for the appropriate level of difficulty. This is likely to be too time consuming for most individual teachers, so I would recommend strongly that groups of teachers work together to build up a bank of test tasks and collectively check that these tasks work in the right way.

Don Snow

Don Snow has an MA in English/TESOL (Michigan State University, 1983) and a PhD in East Asian Language and Cultures (Indiana University, 1991). He was executive director of the English Language Center at Shantou University from 2011 to 2014 and since 2014 has been director of the Language and Culture Center at Duke Kunshan University. His works on language teaching include *More Than a Native Speaker* (TESOL Press, 3rd edition 2017; with Maxi Campbell), *From Language Learner to Language Teacher* (TESOL Press, 2007) and *Encounters with Westerners: Improving Skills in English* and *Intercultural Communication* (Shanghai Foreign Language Education Press, revised edition 2014).

Go beyond What Is Required in English Class

An Interview with Dr. Don Snow

Reporter: As you said in your speech, students in China usually have to resort to independent study to improve their English speaking skills, but the problem is that not all students have the resources or are willing to be engaged in independent study. What do you think can be improved in the current English teaching curriculum in China, so that every student can be engaged and practice their speaking?

Don Snow: First, to be perfectly honest, I'm not sure that we can get every student excited about English learning, but I do think we can increase the number who are interested and engaged. I think we can also do more to help students develop a good understanding of what success in language learning requires. I think it's important for us to tell them that if they really want to learn to speak and listen well, they need to go beyond what is required in class. I think the message students sometimes think they hear is that if they just do their homework, everything should be OK. But learning a language requires going beyond what's required in class. In English classes, we're not just teaching English—we are teaching students how to learn a language—and this includes helping them develop reasonable expectations and strategies.

Reporter: How do you think English educators and learners benefit from this assembly?

Don Snow: In our teaching work, it's just so easy to focus all the time on the courses that we've been teaching for a long time. We kind of get into a rut. We may not even have a lot of time to talk to our colleagues, right? But in the conference here, during presentations, you're exposed to many new ideas. You also have a chance to talk to other people and see how they face the same challenges you do. So this is a wonderful cross-fertilization opportunity. And I think learners also benefit because they get teachers who come back from a conference like this equipped with new ideas and recharged with energy and enthusiasm for teaching.

Reporter: How do you think the assembly encourages exchanges of ideas in English education between China and the rest of the world?

Don Snow: I think this conference is a very important opportunity and channel through which language educators in China can exchange ideas with language educators in other parts of the world. China has the world's largest English teaching industry. English teaching is a huge, important thing here. And there are obviously many exchanges that can go on just within the Chinese English teaching community. But it's also wonderful if such cross-fertilization can involve both language educators from English-speaking countries and from other countries where English is not the first language. Frankly, I think it's also important to bring in people who are teaching and learning languages other than English. The more perspectives that we come at the language learning issue from, the more we can learn, and the better we can perform as professionals.

Reporter: What do you think about the similarities and differences of English language education between China and US?

Don Snow: The first and most obvious difference lies in the language environment. Students learning English in the US are surrounded by English and—at least in theory— should have many opportunities to practice using it. In contrast, English is used much less outside the classroom in China and there are fewer naturally-occurring chances to use it, so learners need to be much more pro-active in finding opportunities to use and practice English. The good news is that in today's China, if learners make an effort to do so, they generally can find opportunities to practice listening to, reading, and even speaking and writing English. I should also add that even when Chinese students are in the US, they often need to be quite pro-active about looking for English practice opportunities, because actually it is often possible even in the US for Chinese speakers to spend much of their time in Chinese-speaking communities. Reaching out beyond those communities generally requires a degree of intentional effort.

A second difference has to do with the degree and kind of motivation learners have. In China a large part of the English-learning population consists of students who are studying English because it is required in school, and because of the pressure to perform well in English on high-stakes tests such as the National College Entrance Examination (Gao Kao). Of course external motivators such as school requirements and tests can be powerful drivers of English study, and they do ensure that many people devote considerable effort to English study for quite a long time. However, eventually students in China complete their required English courses and tests, and many of them more or less stop working on English after that point, "returning their English to their teachers." In contrast, while learners in the US may also study in part because of required English courses and/or tests, many learners also have additional motivators, such as the desire to study in English-medium universities or perhaps get jobs in companies where English is widely used. What this difference means for students learning English in China is that they need to be careful not to let examination success be their only motivation for studying English, and they need to consciously develop motivation strategies that will drive on-going study and use of English even after they have completed all their required courses and tests.

A final difference has to do with what I will call learning targets. As mentioned, students of English in China often study mainly in order to take and pass various kinds of English examinations. While such examinations generally do test language skills—reading, listening, speaking and writing—they tend to focus quite heavily on grammar and vocabulary, and this encourages learners to devote much of their attention and study time to the elements of the language itself; in contrast, skills such as writing and especially speaking count for less, mainly because testing these skills is hard when there are a large number of students. So English courses often devote relatively large amounts of class time to vocabulary and grammar, and don't invest enough time in language practice. The result is that many learners know large amounts of vocabulary and know quite a bit about grammar rules, but haven't had enough English skill practice so that they can use English confidently and effectively.

In contrast, learners in the US often have a very clear picture in their minds of what they will need to do in English—what skills they will need. For example, students preparing for graduate programs in US universities know they will need to read articles, give presentations, engage in classroom discussions, write papers, and so forth. In other words, they have vivid English-learning goals that involve not only knowing the language but using it for real-life purposes, and this increases the chances that learners will study and practice language skills in ways that prepare them for actual use of the language.

Of course it is also possible for learners in China to prepare themselves for actual use of English—and a great many do so. However, this often requires that they go above and beyond the requirements of school English courses and find additional ways to practice English skills. And in order to sustain "independent language study" of this kind, they need to have clear, concrete goals that guide and drive them—a vision of their future English use that focuses on actual use rather than just language study itself.

Reporter: You mentioned that virtually all good English learners in China had engaged in various forms of independent language learning. What do you think teachers should do to foster students' autonomy in learning English?

Don Snow: One thing teachers can do to build learner autonomy is, when assigning homework, to explain to students both how they should practice and what the benefits of practicing that way are. For example, when assigning students to read a passage in a textbook, it only takes a minute or so to explain how you want students to go about reading the passage—what steps and in what order—and why you suggest they do it that way. (I often encourage students to first read a passage without studying the new vocabulary, in order to practice guessing. Then I suggest they study the new vocabulary and read the passage again, with help from the additional clues provided by the new words.) Explaining how you want students to study is a fairly simple approach—and doesn't take much time—but it is a good first step in getting students started thinking about the study strategies they use.

Another thing teachers can do to foster autonomy is to use homework assignments as an opportunity to encourage students to try out different strategies and find out what strategies work best for them. For example, there are many different ways students could go about memorizing a list of new vocabulary words, or studying with the recording of a dialogue, and teachers can suggest two or three different approaches and encourage students to experiment with them. This fosters autonomy by exposing students to more learning strategy ideas, giving them the opportunity to make choices for themselves, and encouraging them to critically evaluate the efficacy of the choices they make.

However, the strategy I find myself using the most often both in class and in after-class conversations is simply telling students stories about various language learning plans, both plans that worked and those that didn't. Many of the stories I tell are drawn from my own experience as a language learner, but I also make a point of asking other people about their experiences, and many of the stories I tell come from the experiences of others. Of course we need to be a little careful about the messages we send by telling stories. For example, if I tell students about some strategy that helped me improve my listening comprehension, I don't want to give them the impression that the approach I used is necessarily the "best" or "right" approach, Instead, I want to be very clear that my goal is to share an idea—a strategy that was helpful (or not helpful) for me, which they might also try out to see if it helps them too.

The key thing here is that the stories I tell don't all revolve around required language courses; in fact, most have to do with language learning plans that go beyond what is required in courses. That gives the stories two purposes. The first and most obvious one is to share ideas about how one might go about building skills in a new language. But the other equally important purpose is to get learners thinking about things they could do on their own—rather than just things required by courses—to pursue success in language learning. Based on both my own experience and my knowledge of the research on language learning, I think it is safe for us to assume that learners have a much greater chance of ultimate success in language learning if they pro-actively engage in one or more forms of independent language learning.

Chuang Wang

Chuang Wang is Distinguished Professor and Dean of the Faculty of Education at the University of Macau. His expertise includes applied statistics and English language learner's self-efficacy beliefs. He has published more than 180 books, book chapters, journal articles, and conference proceedings. He received the 2008 American Educational Research Association Distinguished Paper Award and the Excellent in Teaching Award as well as The Harshini V. de Silva Graduate Mentor Award at the University of North Carolina at Charlotte. He served as the Editor-in-Chief of two peer-reviewed journals and the President of the Chinese American Educational Research and Development Association (2008–2010).

Keep a Balance between Teaching, Research and Service

An interview with Professor Chuang Wang

Reporter: I would like to start off on a more personal note, Professor Wang. May I firstly invite you to talk (briefly) about your academic and professional life highlighting how you become interested in your focal areas (e. g. Quantitative Research Methods/Applied Statistics/Applied Linguistics) of research?

Chuang Wang: Let's start with applied linguistics. I was interested in the English language when I was in middle school. I became fascinated with the English language because that was the first foreign language I learned. I believed that it was cool to be able to speak a language other than my native language. I built up my self-esteem and self-confidence gradually with my success in learning English. My performance on English language test was almost always Number 1 among all my cohorts in my middle and high schools. When it is time for me to choose my major at college, I decided to apply for the English for Science and Technology program at Xi'an Jiaotong University as an engineering student with a very high performance in mathematics. I did not choose mathematics as my major because I did not know what I could do with a degree in mathematics. During my doctoral study at the Ohio State University in the United States, I was asked to do some data analyses for my supervisor, which opened the door of statistics to me. I started to take statistics courses to help me analyze the data but soon was attracted by the power of statistics. I took more statistics courses in the statistics department and received a master's degree. After my graduation from the Ohio State University, I became an assistant professor at the University of North Carolina at Charlotte teaching quantitative research methods. The more I taught quantitative research methods, the more I was attracted by it because I felt the joy of helping my students understand research design and use statistics in their teaching.

Reporter: You have conducted a lot of research on individual differences (e. g. self-efficacy, motivation, enjoyment, and anxiety) in English Education/ Language Education. Can you tell us a bit more about what got you interested in these specific topics, what your research has found, and how your findings can help teachers and learners?

Chuang Wang: I became interested in individual differences when I was working for my supervisor, Dr. Stephen Pape, at the Ohio State University, on a grant with a focus on middle school students' use of self-regulated learning strategies in solving mathematical word problems. Since I had quite a few years of experience teaching English and had a master's degree in applied linguistics, I brought up the idea to investigate English language learners' use of self-regulated learning strategies in learning English. With his encouragement, I explored more related topics, such as self-efficacy, motivation, resilience, and anxiety. This is how I got into this field.

Results from my research suggested that affective attributes such as self-efficacy and motivation as well as strategic behaviors such as self-regulation are related to academic achievement. In particular, English language learners with a strong motivation and high level of self-efficacy are more likely to take challenges, be persistent when they meet difficulties, and feel less anxious when studying the English language. My studies also suggest that higher achievers in the English language acquisition are more likely to use a variety of self-regulated learning strategies when pursing their academic goals.

The implication of my research findings suggests that teachers of English should recognize individual differences and help their students develop self-regulated learning strategies that best enhance their learning of the language.

Reporter: Most of your empirical research has focused on self-efficacy. What does this individual difference variable refer to? Why is it important? How can English language teachers enhance EFL/ESL learners' self-efficacy (if at all possible)? How can English language learners themselves improve their own self-efficacy (if at all possible)?

Chuang Wang: Self-efficacy is close to self-confidence but different in that it is more context specific, task specific, and malleable. It refers to one's beliefs in how well he/she can accomplish a specific task with the assessment of his/her own capabilities. For example, "My English is good" is not self-efficacy, but "I can introduce myself in English" is self-efficacy. It is important in learning because students are more likely to persist in learning and are more likely to employ self-regulated learning strategies with high levels of self-efficacy.

English language teachers can enhance EFL/ESL learners' self-efficacy through the four sources of self-efficacy identified by Bandura: mastery experience, vicarious experience, feedback, and emotional states. In particular, teachers of English are also encouraged to help students enhance their self-efficacy beliefs by giving students tasks that they can achieve so that they can build up their confidence in learning, asking them to observe their peers performing on the English language tasks, giving them constructive feedback, and making the class more fun so that students can learn English in a relaxed and joyful atmosphere. Language learning should be fun.

Reporter: Based on your research concerning EFL/ESL learners' individual differences, can you please share with us the takeaways?

Chuang Wang: I would like to share two messages: (1) there are individual differences. Teachers are encouraged to recognize individual differences of their students and help individual students enhance their self-efficacy beliefs so that they are motivated to learn and persist in learning; and (2) strategies matter. There are certain strategies that are associated with success in academic achievement, but the most important takeaway message is that students need to be the active agent. They have to be able to set their goals, reflect on their performance, and adjust their goals and strategies when necessary. Spending time alone is not enough for learning.

Reporter: When your research subjects included very young learners, did you have any difficulties/challenges in soliciting the cooperation of your research subjects? How did you overcome these difficulties/challenges?

Chuang Wang: Yes, I worked with first-grade and second-grade students in elementary schools for my dissertation and encountered quite a lot of challenges. For example, young learners would not understand the Likert scale in a survey study. I used some smiling faces for them to indicate endorsement of my statement. To observe their use of self-regulated learning strategies in learning English, I videotaped them during their play and asked them follow-up questions based on my analysis of their behaviors on the video. The attention span of young learners is short, so I had to use multiple visits instead of a single visit to their families.

Reporter: Much of your research concerns the instrument validation/ development/modification. Many novice researchers (e. g. postgraduate students) seem to believe that creating their own research instruments (e. g. a questionnaire) is easy. In connection with this belief, can you please provide some tips by means of sharing several concrete examples?

Chuang Wang: I have to say that creating one's own research instrument is not easy. For example, when I was creating my self-efficacy questionnaire, I did a lot of research into this topic before creating the items. I reviewed all existing instruments that were relevant and had to justify why none of them could meet the needs of my study. After the justification of the needs, I adapted some items from existing instruments and created some new items, piloted the questionnaire with a sample, interviewed some students and teachers of English for their opinions on the appropriateness and easiness-to-understand. Then, I did a series of studies on the psychometric properties, such as reliability, validity, invariance across gender and culture, item difficulty, item discrimination.

Reporter: Prior to coming to Macau, you worked in University of North Carolina at Charlotte (UNC-Charlotte, USA), for 15 years, where you had

served as Director for the Ph. D. Programme in Educational Research, Measurement and Evaluation. Can you share with us the interesting/challenging bits of your experience of working in the USA?

Chuang Wang: Sure. I worked in the USA for 15 years at UNC Charlotte and served as the Inaugural Director for the Ph. D. program in Educational Research, Measurement and Evaluation. Overall, I enjoyed my work because I could focus on my research and teaching with the support from my university and family. My university provided me with a platform and resources for conducting research studies that fall into my own interests. I had a freedom to choose whatever topics I would like to explore. For example, I was interested in learning English as a second language and digital citizenship because I would like to help my own children in the schools. I was able to secure funding to support my research and my publications in these fields, which counted toward my tenure and promotion. I have a feeling that I was paid to do the things that I like. The challenges that I met working in the US was my identity as a Chinese scholar. As many other Chinese scholars may agree, we were viewed as hardworking and intelligent. Most American colleagues, however, did not view me as a leader. That was why I tried to lead the doctoral program in my department in order to show my leadership skills. The biggest challenge that I met while working in the US is the opportunity to become a leader as a Chinese scholar.

Reporter: In your current position as Dean of Faculty of Education in the University of Macau (Macau SAR, China), do you need to develop/lead a similar doctoral programme in the broad area of educational research? What are your visions for the new programme(s) at your current institution? What challenges do you need to address?

Chuang Wang: Yes. As soon as I took the position as Dean of the Faculty of Education in the University of Macau, I started a new doctoral program: Doctor of Education (Ed. D.). That program is different from a Ph. D. program in that it is more practice-oriented and targets educational leaders. We have now successfully recruited two cohorts of 60 Ed. D. students in our faculty. My visions for this new program are to make a connection between theory and practice and to train educational leaders for Pre-K-12 schools in Macau SAR of China, the Greater Bay area, and other parts of China.

Reporter: You have vast teaching, research and administrative experiences spanning over your academic career. How compatible do you find these different roles? To what extent is it necessary for a novice faculty member to get engaged in research and administration in addition to teaching?

Chuang Wang: We all need to keep a balance between teaching, research, and service. To me, these are all important and connected. For example, I teach statistics to education major graduate students and I use statistics in my research and my review of manuscripts for journals. I used to spend 50% of my time on research, 30% of my time on teaching, and 20% of my time on service when I was working as a faculty member. However, I now spend approximately 60% of my time on service as the Dean of the Faculty of Education in the University of Macau.

In my opinion, a novice faculty member should spend most of the time on research in addition to teaching. Service is not a priority for a novice faculty member, so some minimal required service for the department and university is sufficient. I do not encourage a novice faculty member to be actively engaged in community service.

Reporter: You also are an editorial member of quite a few international applied linguistics journals. What are some of the challenges you have faced in your editorship member role?

Chuang Wang: The biggest challenge is to find responsible reviewers for the journal. Another challenge is the lack of quality papers at the beginning. I worked as the Editor for a new journal and I tried very hard to encourage people to submit their quality papers to me. This is like a chicken-and-egg dilemma. In order to attract scholars to send their quality papers to a journal, the journal needs to be well-recognized in the field. However, a new journal needs quality papers to become recognized in academia.

Reporter: Thanks to the globalization, we are having more and more contact with people who are culturally different. In your opinion, what are the important

factors for successful cross-cultural communication? Does English education play a role in communicating Chinese opinions/experiences/solutions to the world?

Chuang Wang: Emotional intelligence or communication skills are important for successful cross-cultural communication. We need to respect people from a different culture and make sure we understand their ways of communication and behaviors. English education plays a significant role in communicating Chinese opinions/experiences/solutions to the world because English is the dominant media of communication in the world.

Reporter: Finally, what is on the horizon for you? Are there any particular areas of teaching and research that you are interested in and excited about?

Chuang Wang: I am currently interested in experimental or quasi-experimental studies to examine the sources of self-efficacy beliefs and the impacts of self-efficacy beliefs in learning English as a foreign language. I hope these experimental or quasi-experimental studies may help answer some questions about the causal relationships between self-efficacy and other affective measures and academic achievements.